REPUTATION
MANAGEMENT

REPUTATION MANAGEMENT

The Future of Corporate Communications and Public Relations

PRCA Practice Guides

Written and curated by

TONY LANGHAM
FCIPR, MPRCA

United Kingdom — North America — Japan
India — Malaysia — China

Emerald Publishing Limited
Howard House, Wagon Lane, Bingley BD16 1WA, UK

First edition 2019

British Library Cataloguing in Publication Data
A catalogue record for this book is available from the British
Library

ISBN:978-1-78756-610-1 (Print)
ISBN:978-1-78756-607-1 (Online)
ISBN:978-1-78756-609-5 (Epub)

ISOQAR certified
Management System,
awarded to Emerald
for adherence to
Environmental
standard
ISO 14001:2004.

Certificate Number 1985
ISO 14001

INVESTOR IN PEOPLE

This book is dedicated to all of the colleagues, clients and other friends who've made Lansons what it is today — and to Clare, Alex and Theo, who've made it all worthwhile.

CONTENTS

LIST OF TABLES

LIST OF DIAGRAMS

FOREWORD

Reputation Management: The Future of Corporate Communications and Public Relations is part of the *PRCA Practice Guides* series. Each is a uniquely practical and readable guide, providing PR and communications professionals, new and experienced alike, with hands-on guidance to manage in the field. Written by experienced practitioners who have been there and done it, *PRCA Practice Guides* offer powerful insights into the challenges of the modern industry and guidance on how to navigate your way through them.

This book gives senior executives and communications professionals the arguments to emphasise the importance of reputation – how positively or negatively an organisation is perceived by stakeholders such as employees, customers, Government and members of the media – and inspires their thinking in managing reputation. Opinions vary widely on what reputation is and how it is created, and there is no accepted model for managing and protecting reputation – is it merely "PR" – or is it a key Board responsibility? The book is intended as a practical guide and includes essays, interviews and check-lists produced by some of the world's leading thinkers on reputation management – including business leaders, celebrities and communications professionals.

Tony Langham is one of the UK's leading reputation management and public relations professionals. As well as retaining a hands-on role with clients, he has contributed significantly to the promotion of our industry. The firm he co-founded, Lansons, has built a reputation for leadership in award-winning work, ethical conduct, employee ownership and gender equality. I'm delighted that he agreed to contribute to this series.

Francis Ingham
Director General, PRCA
Chief Executive, ICCO

ABOUT THE AUTHOR

Tony Langham is an adviser, entrepreneur and Chairman with over 35 years' front-line experience fighting for the reputations of companies, organisations and governments.

In 1989, he and Clare Parsons co-founded Lansons by remortgaging their London flat and taking out a string of credit cards. Tony is still Chief Executive of Lansons, now a leading reputation management consultancy that has been named 'UK Agency of the Year' on 17 occasions. Lansons has won over 70 industry awards and for the last 14 years has been named as one of the 50 best medium-sized businesses to work for in the UK. In 2017, it was the Public Relations and Communications Association's (PRCA) first ever 'Very Large Agency Ethical Champion'.

Tony also holds senior Non-executive Chairman roles in the financial technology, market research and horse racing industries.

PR Week named him as one of the 300 most influential PR professionals in the world in its Global Power Book in 2016 and 2017.

In 2014 and 2015 Debrett's named Tony as one of the 500 most influential people in the UK and in 2016, he received the Mark Mellor award for outstanding contribution to the UK public relations industry from the PRCA.

He is a regular writer, commentator and conference speaker. *Reputation Management: The Future of Corporate Communications and Public Relations* is his first book.

Email: tonyl@lansons.com

Twitter: @TonyLangham   LinkedIn: http://uk.linkedin.com/in/tonylangham

ABOUT THE CONTRIBUTORS

Iain Anderson is an expert in public policy and complex corporate communications issues. He has also worked for a range of UK politicians and was part of the founding team at Cicero Group. His current clients include FTSE 100 and Fortune 500 companies across a range of industry sectors.

He regularly contributes to Sky News and BBC. Iain is non-Executive Director of Innovate Finance, Patron of the National Portrait Gallery and Stonewall Ambassador. Iain is former Chairman of the Association of Professional Political Consultants.

Dr Helena Boschi is a Psychologist who focuses on applied neuroscience in the work place. Her particular areas of interest include the brain and behaviour, our emotional and rational neural networks and how to improve our cognitive abilities in order to get the best out of our own and others' brainpower.

Helena has held senior talent management and organisation development positions within international companies and now works across a range of industries worldwide. Her work with her clients involves designing new and creative learning initiatives, particularly in the areas of leadership and team development, intercultural communication and organisational change.

With a deep commitment to ongoing research in psychology, neuroscience and behaviour, Helena possesses keen insight into best and evolving practices in learning, communication and leadership. As member of the British Psychological Society, she brings a scientific edge to the work she delivers, delivered in a way that is easy to understand and apply.

Emily Dickinson joined Opinium in January 2018 after working for Kantar Millward Brown where she led innovation, development and marketing for the Corporate and Healthcare practices. As a former freelance journalist and editor, Emily specialises in engaging with B2B and B2C audiences on behalf of both private and public-sector clients to help shape communication strategies, evaluate market trends and increase the strategic responsiveness of their organisations.

Emily holds a PhD in American Literature and is advisory board member for Loughborough University's Online Civic Culture Centre for Doctoral Training.

John Doorley headed corporate communication at Merck & Co., Inc. until 2000. He then began a career of teaching, reputation management scholarship, and consulting on that emerging discipline.

He built and taught the world's first undergraduate course in reputation management at Rutgers University and then the world's first such graduate course, at New York University. He holds the IP on the Comprehensive Reputation Management process. He co-authored the first text on *Reputation Management* (2006), the 4th edition of which will be released in early 2019.

In 2015, John joined the full-time faculty as a visiting Associate Professor in the School of Communications at Elon University, ranked #1 nationally in the United States in programmes focused on student success.

Steve Earl is Managing Director, Europe, at Zeno Group, the fast-growing, mid-sized global communications agency helping brands to communicate more creatively and courageously. Zeno acquired London's 3 Monkeys in 2016 to create 3 Monkeys | Zeno in the UK.

As well as his work on the commercial side, Steve advises clients on media technique, brand behaviour and personal reputation.

He began his career as a news journalist before moving into public relations. Steve co-founded, managed and sold two award-winning public relations agencies with Stephen Waddington: Rainier PR in 1998 and Speed in 2009.

Richard Edelman is the President and CEO of Edelman, the leading communications marketing firm, located in over 60 cities with more than 6,000 employees worldwide. Richard has extensive experience in marketing and reputation management, having led assignments with major corporations, NGOs and family businesses in over 25 industries around the world. He has counselled countries in every region of the world on economic development programmes.

As the creator of the annual Edelman Trust Barometer, Richard has become one of the foremost authorities on trust in business, government, media and NGOs. Under Richard's leadership, the agency has garnered many of the industry's top accolades. Richard, has also earned many industry honours. He topped *PRWeek*'s list of most powerful executives (2013), was recognized as the third highest-rated CEO by Glassdoor (2014) and was inducted in the Arthur W. Page Society's Hall of Fame (2014) among others.

Richard serves on the Board of Directors of the Ad Council, the Atlantic Council, the Chicago Council on Global Affairs, the Children's Aid Society, the Gettysburg Foundation, the 9/11 Museum and the National Committee on US China Relations. He is Commissioner on The Business Commission and Member of the World Economic Forum and PR Seminar. Richard earned his MBA from Harvard Business School in 1978 and a Bachelor of Arts from Harvard College in 1976.

Winfried Engelbrecht-Bresges, GBS JP, joined The Hong Kong Jockey Club in 1998 and has been its Chief Executive Officer since 2007. Under his leadership the Club has undergone significant transformation, developing its customer-centricity, becoming one of the world's top 10 charity donors, as well as raising the quality and profile of Hong Kong racing to a world-class standard.

Internationally, Mr Engelbrecht-Bresges serves as Vice Chairman of the International Federation of Horseracing Authorities, the world's highest thoroughbred racing authority, and is Chairman of the Asian Racing Federation. He is also a member of the Advisory Board of Aachen-Laurensberger Rennverein e.V. which is the organiser of the World Equestrian Festival, CHIO Aachen.

Simon English is the Senior City Correspondent of the *Evening Standard*. He also writes the widely read *Tomorrow's Business* newsletter produced by Roxhill and Signal.

Simon has been a financial journalist for more than 20 years. He started at the *Sunday Telegraph* in 1996, later moving to the *Daily Telegraph*. He was in New York correspondent for five years, covering 9/11 and the corporate scandals of the early 2000s' including Enron.

He was later City Editor of *The Sun* and is now on his second stint at the *London Evening Standard*.

Stephen Hahn-Griffiths is a strategic thought-leader, and purveyor of insight related to corporate brand reputation measurement, monitoring and management. At Reputation

Institute, he is a vanguard of the organisation's proprietary reputation measurement model — RepTrak®. Stephen oversees Reputation Institute's extensive global reputation research programme including the RT100 study featured in Forbes. His realm of expertise includes corporate reputation management, brand purpose and CSR.

His work in reputation, integrated communications and brand strategy has been critically acclaimed — and he has won major industry awards, including EFFIEs, Clios, Cannes Lions and the Jay Chiat Award for Strategic Excellence. His academic credentials include an MBA from New York University, and Dip. Ad from Watford College.

He is often cited as a reputation expert and has been quoted in leading news and business media such *ABC*, *NBC*, *Forbes*, *WSJ*, *CNBC*, *NPR*, *Associated Press*, *Adage*, *PRWeek*, *Financial Times*, and *Bloomberg*.

Paul Holmes has been writing, speaking and thinking about public relations for more than 30 years. In 1990, he founded the now-defunct magazine *Reputation Management*. Today, he is founder and chair of The Holmes Group, an online publishing, awards and events company.

Anthony Horowitz is the author of the number one bestselling *Alex Rider* books and the *Power of Five* series. He has enjoyed huge success as a writer for both children and adults. After the success of his first James Bond novel, *Trigger Mortis* (2015), he was invited back by the Ian Fleming Estate to write a second, *Forever and a Day* (2018). His latest crime novel *The Word Is Murder* (2017), introducing detective Daniel Hawthorne, was a *Sunday Times* bestseller. He has won numerous awards, including the Bookseller Association/ Nielsen Author of the Year Award, the Children's Book of the Year Award at the British Book Awards and the Red House Children's Book Award. Anthony has also created and written many major television series, including *Collision*, *New Blood* and the BAFTA-winning *Foyle's War*. He lives in London with his wife, two sons and his dog, Boss.

Fu Jing now works as Managing Director of Beijing-based China Watch Institute, a communication-led think tank platform powered by *China Daily* after working in Brussels for seven and a half years as deputy chief of the media group's European Union bureau. Fu Jing has recently moved to Beijing though he still writes columns for *China Daily*. Their platform www.chinawatch.cn is pending launch at the time of this book's publication.

Dave King founded and runs online reputation management and intelligence business Digitalis, a unique technology firm monitoring and mitigating online risk for high-profile political, commercial and private individuals and corporations. Included in the *Evening Standard's* 2017 list of the 1,000 most influential people in the UK, Dave has advised many global organisations on digital strategies, reputational and cyber risk. He co-authored *Online Publication Claims: A Practical Guide* (2017), the de facto solicitor's handbook in this area. He is a regular media commentator and is listed in the Spears 500 and the Spears Reputation Index. He is Advisor to Concordia and his hypothesis on online recruitment by extremists has been pivotal in framing highly influential research by the Tony Blair Institute for Global Change.

With a background in finance and journalism, **Chris Lewis** has worked for a variety of international and national media. The agency he founded has grown to 500 staff in 30 offices globally. Chris is an experienced strategist and works closely with senior politicians, business leaders and celebrities. He is a donor to a number of organisations including the UK's leading scientific organisation The Royal Society and Chelsea

College of Art & Design, a part of the University of the Arts, London.

He is the author of the best-seller on creativity *Too Fast to Think*. In 2016, working with US Presidential Adviser, author and economist Dr Pippa Malmgren, he founded the LEWIS Advisory Board (LAB). Together, they are co-authors of the 2018 book *The Leadership Lab − Understanding Leadership in the 21st Century*.

William Lewis was appointed Chief Executive Officer of Dow Jones and Publisher of *The Wall Street Journal* in May 2014. He previously served as Chief Creative Officer for News Corp, the parent company of Dow Jones, where he was responsible for the company's creative strategy and developing new commercial opportunities.

Prior to joining News Corp, Mr Lewis served as Editor-in-Chief of Telegraph Media Group, which he joined in 2005. Under his editorship, *The Daily Telegraph* was named UK Newspaper of the Year in the 2010 British Press Awards. This followed the paper's exposure of the parliamentary expenses scandal.

Nitin Mantri is the Group CEO of Avian WE, one of the top three public relations firms in India. He is also the President of the Public Relations Consultants Association of India (PRCAI), the apex body of communications and public relations consultancies in India.

Nitin was appointed Vice-President of The International Communications Consultancy Organisation (ICCO) in 2017. He is the first Indian to hold this prestigious position and will take over as ICCO President in 2019.

Nitin is also the first Indian to receive the PR Leader of the Year Award at the 2015 ICCO Global Awards. Under his leadership, Avian WE has become one of the top 10 fastest-growing consultancies in the world (The Holmes Report

2017), and has won honours like the Independent Agency of the Year title at the ICCO Global Awards 2017, the PR Consultancy of the Year – Large award at Fulcrum Awards 2017, The Best National Agency to Work for by the Holmes Report in 2016.

Dr Caroline Marchant is a Lecturer at University of Edinburgh Business School. Following 10 years in financial services marketing and corporate communications, Caroline undertook marketing consultancy work and teaching at Edinburgh and Heriot Watt Universities, eventually becoming a full-time academic in 2012.

Dame Helena Morrissey is well known in the City, particularly for her work on gender equality. She founded the 30% Club, a campaign for more gender-balanced boards and is chair of the Diversity Project. She joined LGIM in 2017.

Helena has been named one of *Fortune* magazine's World's 50 Greatest Leaders and the *Financial Times*' 2017 'Person of the Year'. She was appointed a Dame in the Queen's 2017 Birthday Honours list.

Helena is a Philosophy graduate. Her first book *A Good Time to be a Girl, Don't Lean In, Change the System* was published in February 2018.

James Nicandrou is Research Executive at Opinium focusing on PR and communications research. Since graduating with a degree in business management, James has focused his attention on using insight to help brands navigate their current and future challenges both in the UK and internationally.

He is the author of Opinium thought leadership pieces of *Streaming: The Future of Entertainment* and *Data Powered Health*.

Matthew Painter is Managing Director of the Ipsos MORI Reputation Centre and Member of the firm's Public Affairs

Management Board. He leads a team of 30 based in Ipsos MORI's London HQ, which helps business leaders to measure and manage their corporate reputation, brand and communications effectiveness. Previously Head of Research at Echo Research Ltd, over 15 years Matt has worked with some of the world's most admired businesses and public sector organisations across Europe, the US, Japan, Russia and the GCC. (matthew.painter@ipsos.com)

Robert Phillips is the author of *Trust Me, PR Is Dead* (Unbound, 2015) and a Visiting Professor at Cass Business School. He is the Co-founder of Jericho Chambers and former UK and EMEA Chief Executive of Edelman, the world's largest Public Relations firm. Robert advises global business leaders and organisations on trust, leadership and communications and is a provocative public speaker and commentator. He has been trying to make the world a better place since the age of eight. *Management Today* calls Robert 'the repentant spinner'.

Danny Rogers is one of the world's pre-eminent media and marketing journalists. He has been Editor of *Campaign* and *PR Week* and is currently Editor-in-Chief of *PR Week UK*. He has won many industry awards including the British Society of Magazine Editors' 'Editor of the Year' in 2008. Rogers has also been a contributing editor to *The Independent, The Guardian* and *Financial Times' Creative Business* and writes a regular column in the *i* newspaper. In 2015, Rogers wrote the seminal book, *Campaigns That Shook the World: The Evolution of Public Relations*. He is a regular speaker at companies and universities worldwide, including Boston University, MA.

James Stevens is a Research Executive at Opinium Research. While James works on a range of B2C and B2B studies across a number of sectors, he has a keen interest in how reputation impacts a company's bottom line. He has experience in helping clients harness the power of insight to improve and promote a company's reputation, having worked alongside the Public Relations and Communications Association, PROI Worldwide and the International Communications Consultancy Organisation.

Arun Sudhaman is CEO and Editor-in-Chief at the Holmes Report, overseeing the Holmes Report's global content offering, including its analysis and insight into reputation, public relations and communications trends and issues. Since joining in 2010, Arun has led a comprehensive relaunch of the title's content platform, including its digital presence and new products such as the Influence 100 compendium of key global influencers, the Global Communications Report, the landmark Creativity in PR study and the Echo Chamber podcast.

Arun has also played a pivotal role expanding the Holmes Report's coverage into Asia-Pacific and other emerging markets, and has helped steer the company's international events programme, particularly the Global Public Relations Summit. Prior to joining the Holmes Report, Arun spent more than seven years with Haymarket Media in Hong Kong, Singapore and London.

In 2015, Arun was inducted into the ICCO Hall of Fame.

Lara Thomas has been a communications consultant for four years at Lansons, specialising in reputation management and strategy. Clients have brought Lara into crisis and issues management, change and employee engagement, political advisory and public affairs and media relations. Lara has worked with clients to navigate reputational risks stemming from policy change, NHS announcements and decision making, health and safety incidents, media and political criticism, stakeholder conflicts of interest and global redundancy programmes.

Lara holds a BA in Geography from the University of Leeds, UK.

Basil Towers is Senior Managing Director at Teneo Blue Rubicon. He researches and advises on reputation in an organisational and functional capability. His 15-year research programme in Europe, the US and EMEA informs the development of proprietary models and benchmarks.

He founded Hesleden Partners in 2005 to help companies manage reputations that deliver business value. It was acquired by Teneo Blue Rubicon in 2014.

Basil started at Burson Marsteller before establishing Shandwick Communications and joining the Shandwick UK board. He set up Christow Consultants, a communications and research consultancy, in 1989 and established the Corporate Affairs Academy in partnership with the Saïd Business School's Centre for Corporate Reputation in 2012.

Kasper Ulf Nielsen is Chief Product Officer at Reputation Institute. Kasper is responsible for designing, developing and implementing the products and services that guide companies on their reputation journey.

Since 2004, Kasper has played a leading role in the development of Reputation Institute into the global leader of reputation measurement and management. Kasper has consulted companies from across 20 + industries in 30 + countries on how to measure and manage their reputation.

As a thought leader in reputation management, Kasper was instrumental in designing the Global RepTrak® study, which is the largest study of corporate reputation in the world. Kasper has developed the Reputation Excellence Framework, which identifies the competencies needed to manage reputation.

Kasper is a frequent commentator on reputation topics in the media, and has been featured in *The Wall Street Journal*, *Forbes*, *Financial Times*, *Bloomberg*, as well as local radio and TV around the world.

Kasper holds a Master of Science in Intercultural Management from Copenhagen Business School with MBA credits from McGill University in Canada.

Stephen Waddington is Partner and Chief Engagement Officer at Ketchum helping clients and colleagues to do the best job possible at engaging with the public.

He is Visiting Professor in Practice at the Newcastle University supporting the university and students through teaching and mentoring.

Stephen originally trained as a journalist before following a career in public relations. He co-founded, managed and sold two award-winning public relations agencies with Steve Earl: Rainier PR in 1998 and Speed in 2009.
Stephen was President of the CIPR in 2014. In 2017, Stephen received the PRCA's outstanding contribution to digital public relations.

David Waller joined FTI Consulting in July 2016 as a Senior Managing Director in the strategic communications practice of FTI Consulting based in London. David has had a 30-year career in financial journalism and communications. He spent nearly 10 years with the *Financial Times*, including a spell as Frankfurt Correspondent and Deputy Head of the Lex Column. Before joining FTI, he was the former Head of Group Communications at Man Group, having previously held senior communications roles at Allianz and Dresdner Kleinwort.

David is a published author on the subjects of both business and PR and his latest work, co-authored with Rupert

Younger, is *The Reputation Game* (2017). For further details see www.davidwallerwriter.com

As a Senior Teaching Fellow at the University of Birmingham, **Hazel Westwood** lectures in PR and Reputation Management. She also consults in reputation building and crisis communications. Following a first career as a journalist, including 18 years on Sky News, Hazel adopts a practitioner's approach, with a nod to peer reviewed research in robust case study analysis. She delivers accessible, practical insights into today's reputational issues, relevant for public, private and third sector organisations. Hazel also leads, designs and develops Business Management programmes in the UK and Singapore, and is Associate of Birmingham Business School's Centre for Responsible Business.

Emma Woollcott is Partner in Mishcon Private and Head of the Reputation Protection Group. She advises individuals, companies and charities on defamation, breach of confidence, invasion of privacy, harassment and data protection concerns. She is particularly adept in digital technology and online publications, often advising in times of crisis and in the context of wider disputes. Emma provides claimants and defendants with pre- and post-publication advice, including obtaining, defending and discharging injunctions. Emma takes a holistic approach to Reputation Protection, encouraging clients to prepare in advance for potential challenges, and effectively mitigating any damage caused by negative publicity.

PREFACE

A good reputation is one of the keys to success in business and in life. Organisations with the best reputations outperform rivals in a myriad of tangible ways from recruiting higher quality staff to succeeding with smaller marketing budgets to exerting greater influence over governments.

In the long term, of course, reputation can only be based on reality and behaviour. The only way to be seen as a great company is to be a great company. The only way to be trusted is to be trustworthy. But in the short term, unfairness is around us. There are great companies that are underestimated and there are organisations and people building unfair advantage. That's because some manage reputation better than others.

This book explores reputation and reputation management. It discusses the forces shaping reputation today and looks towards the future. I believe that reputation management is the future of corporate communications and public relations.

In this book, I have chosen to showcase a wide variety of views from across the world. There are 27 essays and eight in-depth interviews with leaders in a wide range of industries. There are also 39 reputation management case studies drawn from leading practitioners in 27 countries across six continents. The book has plenty of statistics, sidebars and opinions from people of all backgrounds. That's how I wanted it, and I hope you like it that way too.

I close the book by suggesting that the very practice of reputation management is a force for good. Our industry is about dialogue and the world is a better place if governments, organisations and companies are talking to each other and explaining why they do what they do. Enjoy.

ACKNOWLEDGEMENTS

Since its formation in 1989, Lansons has employed over 650 people and worked with well over 1,000 clients. Thank you all. I've learnt something from every one of you, and continue to learn from you every day.

My biggest thanks go to Clare Parsons, whose husband I am, and who co-founded Lansons with me all those years ago. Clare still chairs Lansons and is also current chair of Public Relations Organisations International (PROI), the global network of over 75 independently owned consultancies in over 50 countries across the world. She was an invaluable sounding board to me in writing this book.

Huge thanks for helping put the book together go to Emma Read, who helped co-ordinate the essays and interviews and much more and to Megan Sunderland who helped with the reputation management case studies and provided project management support. Thank you also to other Lansons colleagues – Oshin Sharma for editorial and proofreading support and to Tom Baldock, Timo Burbidge, Shirley Collyer, Callum Finch, Joe Greaney, Hugh James, Michael Lach, Sarah Penney, Emma Robinson, Jamie Smith and Michael White for your help.

It's impossible to name you all here, but I'm super grateful to all 81 people who wrote essays, submitted case studies or agreed to be interviewed by me for this book. It would not have been possible without you.

Special thanks go to James Endersby and his team at Opinium Research in London for conducting original market research studies for this book. Thank you also to Matt Cartmell, Deputy Director General of the Public Relations and Communications Association (PRCA) in London for mobilising International Communications Consultancy Organisation (ICCO) members to take part in one of those surveys.

And finally, thank you to the PRCA and to ICCO for commissioning me to write this book. It's been fun to have the opportunity to make contact with so many different people in different organisations across the world.

1

WHAT IS REPUTATION?

Reputation is real and yet not real at the same time.

Everyone who writes about the subject agrees that the only way to have a great reputation is to be a great company. Rolex is currently the company with the best reputation in the world[1]. It can only be the company with the best reputation because it makes great watches. If it didn't make great watches, it couldn't be the company with the best reputation in the world.

Reputation is first and foremost about what an organisation does. What it produces and how it behaves. It is based on reality.

Yet, Rolex could make great watches but not have a great reputation, at least for a period of time.

That's because an organisation's reputation belongs to others. You are whatever other people say you are. As my first boss, Bob Worcester, Founder of MORI (now part of Ipsos MORI) used to say, 'corporate image' is about 'perceptions not facts'. In this sense, reputation is not reality.

Understanding and living with this dichotomy is fundamental to understanding reputation and reputation management. As is understanding that reputation exists. But I'm
getting ahead of myself.

MY FAVOURITE DEFINITION OF REPUTATION

Eminem had it right in his song *The Way I Am*, but I didn't
ask for permission to reproduce that lyric here. In any event,
my favourite definition of reputation comes from John
Doorley who co-authored *Reputation Management*[2] with
Helio Fred Garcia and who I've come to see as the father of
reputation management.

His formula is reproduced in the wonderful essay on pages
71–76. It states that reputation is the sum of images of
others, and it comes from performance plus behaviour plus
communication. And that it can only be sustained if an
organisation is authentic and true to its purpose or to a set of
values.

That says it all.

MULTIPLE REPUTATIONS

However, it's vital to acknowledge that an organisation or
individual can have multiple reputations. Or different reputations with different audiences at the same time. At the time of
writing, the British Virgin Islands (or BVI) has an excellent
reputation with those who set up companies for international
investment, but a less rosy reputation with the European
Union or NGOs (non-governmental organizations) like
Christian Aid.

This aspect of reputation is very well described by David Waller and Rupert Younger in their excellent book, *The Reputation Game* (2017). They split an organisation's 'character reputation' (moral and social qualities) from its 'capability reputation' (fulfilling specific tasks). David updates some of their core arguments in his essay on pages 82−86 of this book.

CHIEF EXECUTIVES, PRESIDENTS AND CELEBRITIES DON'T CARE ABOUT DEFINITIONS

Books on reputation management love to debate definitions, such as the difference between brand and reputation. Senior professionals in traditionally structured companies also love to create silos, debating whether something is the responsibility of corporate communications or public affairs or marketing or HR. In commercial life, caring about definitions or silos is usually in inverse proportion to the importance of the task.

The CEO or President or celebrity doesn't care about definitions, indeed they often blur definitions that academics take for granted. Jeff Bezos, the founder of Amazon, is one of many CEOs to use the phrase 'brand reputation' (Bloomberg, 2004).

Leaders care about being successful. They care about being able to enter a completely new market. Or being able to influence Government more than their rivals. Or being able to win the next starring role. Or negotiating a favourable trade deal. Or being able to increase sales with a relatively low marketing spend.

These things are more readily achieved by those with the magic ingredient that we variously call respect, trust, brand equity, image amongst other things. We all understand implicitly what this is — that seemingly indefinable quality that makes success more likely. That magic ingredient is best described as a reputation. It can be built, maintained, protected, measured and managed.

But before we discuss reputation management, let's first glory in some great reputations and what makes them.

2

WHAT MAKES A GREAT REPUTATION?

In this chapter, we admire some great reputations and probe the foundations beneath them. Nitin Mantri outlines the six keys to a great reputation: retaining the customer's trust, consistent innovation, happy employees, an able leadership team, social responsibility and continuous engagement. Two fabulous essays and two interviews then bring these attributes to life.

At the core of every great reputation is greatness itself. International best-selling author Anthony Horowitz explains the enduring appeal of James Bond, 'a creation of genius' in 1952, who endures to this day. He concludes that in the world of celebrity 'you'll keep your reputation so long as you're loved'.

Holmes Report CEO and Global Editor-in-Chief Arun Sudhaman dissects the importance of Unilever CEO Paul Polman, who has collected a string of international awards and accolades for his commitment to sustainability. Arun echoes Polman's view that 'capitalism can no longer prosper at the expense of society'.

THE DRIVE FOR AUTHENTICITY AND PURPOSE

The drive to be seen as a purpose-driven business is currently the number-one trend in global reputation management. All around the world, Governments, organisations and companies are working hard to convince their staff, their customers and society at large that their very existence benefits everybody. In our jargon-filled world, this drive can be called purpose, vision and values, corporate narrative, storytelling or can even be phrased in plain English: 'Why do we exist?' or 'What are we here for?'

Where these projects are authentic and real, they can be stunningly successful. We believe LEGO, the company with the second-best reputation in the world, when CEO Niels Christiansen says its purpose 'is to inspire and develop the builders of tomorrow' (Reputation Institute Reptrak 100, 2018). One of the most impressive transformations is CEO Indra Nooyi's 'Performance with Purpose' reorganisation at PepsiCo. Badging Pepsi and Doritos as 'fun-for-you' products is credible. There is no 'spin' or unbelievable overclaiming. Diet Pepsi is billed as 'better-for-you' – allowing Tropicana and Quaker Oats to flourish as 'good-for-you' products (ChiefExecutive.net, 2018).

I've been into so many corporate headquarters and seen words like 'integrity' and 'quality service' plastered on the walls, that I have a degree of scepticism over the tsunami of 'purpose projects' currently going on. I fear that many companies will overclaim in their purpose, mission, vision and values. This will actually sow the seeds of future reputational problems when it's discovered that their deeds don't match their fine words.

For this book, I'm delighted to be able to showcase a set of truly authentic values. In my interview with the 11th Duke of Richmond and Gordon – owner of The Goodwood Estate in Sussex, England – he takes me through four core values that fit a business built on the appeal of fast and beautiful cars, planes and horses. If you've ever been bored reading a set of corporate values, I guarantee that you won't be this time.

OBSESSION AND PARANOIA

Many (some would say most) of the world's great businesses have been driven by the vision and passion of one or two people. In the past, this has included Walt Disney in the USA, Jamsetji Tata in India, Masaru Ibuki and Akio Morito (Sony) in Japan. More recently, we think of Bill Gates and Mark Zuckerberg in the USA, Richard Branson in the UK or Jack Ma (Alibaba) in China. This driving force is a key part of many of the world's success stories and these people do not approach their jobs in the same way as the rest of the population.

In this chapter, the two interviews with business owners give some insight into what it takes to drive and transform a business from the top. Britain's most trusted man, Martin Lewis, Founder of Money Saving Expert (MSE), says that his secret is 'paranoia' adding that 'no one is as critical of what we do as I am'. When I put this word to the Duke of Richmond and Gordon, he said he understood it. One of his values is the 'obsession for perfection'. He said that he worries all the time and if anyone has a poor experience at Goodwood 'it's a dagger to the heart'.

SOME COMPANIES CAN'T AFFORD A GOOD REPUTATION

I've sat in meetings, particularly with banks, where it has become clear that it's simply not possible to do what consumer groups and commentators judge to be trustworthy and at the same time meet shareholders' expectations of the business. Martin Lewis touches on the same issue in his interview. His judgement is that

> lots of companies want to be trusted, but are not willing to pay for it and it would be better if they were at least honest with themselves about this.

I think this applies to most areas where competition is intense and confusion marketing predominates, including energy and telecoms. The answer is to not overclaim in describing corporate purpose.

On that note, I'll leave you to read Nitin Mantra on what makes a great reputation, my interview with the Duke of Richmond and Gordon on obsessing for perfection, Arun Sudhaman on Paul Polman and my interview with Martin Lewis, 'Britain's most trusted person'. The chapter is completed by Danny Rogers, Editor-in-Chief, *PR Week* UK and author of *Campaigns That Shook the World: The Evolution of Public Relations* (2015) who writes of his admiration for Dove and John Lewis. I'll re-join you on page 29 to talk about the value of reputation.

WHAT MAKES A GREAT REPUTATION?

Nitin Mantri

Group CEO AvianWE; Vice President, ICCO; President, PRCAI

Reputation is a valuable, strategic asset for every business. Even though it is an intangible concept, reputation gauges the degree of trust that the consumers, clients, marketplace and the industry as a whole, hold for a brand. From driving consumer preference and facilitating growth, to ensuring public support in times of crisis, a good reputation is the most important thing that a company can build and have.

Building a good reputation is not easy. *It requires years of effort, patience and time to build a good reputation* and just one misstep to destroy it. Yet, companies like Rolex, Google, Microsoft and Walt Disney are consistently featured in lists of the world's most reputable organisations. So, what gives these organisations a stellar reputation? Let's find out.

RETAIN THE CUSTOMER'S TRUST

Honesty is the foundation of a good reputation. An organisation that behaves ethically is admirable, trustworthy and worthy of respect. The presence of integrity and transparency in all dealings is an essential ingredient for building an impressive outlook. The maintenance of financial and economic resources should be performed responsibly and without any ambiguity.

The turmoil that Nestlé in India had to endure after Maggi failed to secure FDA approvals inflicted a major dent on the brand's global reputation. However, the brand's constant devotion to their customers with honest assurances and confessions ensured one of the greatest comebacks of all time and great lessons on brand reconstruction.

INNOVATE CONSISTENTLY

The brand that services an irrefutable product quality is bound to be in consumers' good graces. A good personal experience ties an indiscernible string of faith of a consumer to the brand. A token of that would be the consistency in Rolex's brand reputation throughout the years.

To cement their status, Rolex pioneered several industry's firsts, including the first waterproof watch and patenting the self-winding mechanism, as well as others. Upon their twin principles of unwavering product quality and timely innovation, the Swiss watchmaker has built a name for itself.

HAPPY EMPLOYEES

An employee who enjoys working at your company is likely to spread a word about the geniality of your business. Investing in their individual growth will result in greater satisfaction leading to better results. An organisation is nothing but what its employees make it to be and what its consumers deem it to be.

Google's mantra of employee satisfaction has constantly ranked it amongst the best places to work. The implementation of a cheerful work culture and a host of office perks has always made it the yardstick for an ideal employer.

AN ABLE LEADERSHIP TEAM

Great brands always need inspiring leaders to spearhead their way, but no leader is greater than their brand. Last year, when an ex-Uber employee's essay detailing the prevailing culture of sexism and sexual harassment surfaced on the internet, the organisation found itself rushing into an unforeseen predicament. To make matters worse, a video of then-CEO Travis Kalanick berating an Uber driver was also leaked within a few days of that incident. Kalanick was compelled to make a public apology followed by his resignation from Uber.

Reputation is fragile but there is nothing that a well-structured rebuilding cannot beget. Under the guidance of great management and an envisaging leadership team, brand consolidation becomes a promising goal. Microsoft under the leadership of Satya Nadella has done just that and has risen up in most reputation rankings since he took over.

BE SOCIALLY RESPONSIBLE

It is important for a business to communicate on a humane level, while being able to help the society move ahead with the times and as a whole. When a company addresses concerns beyond its anticipated role, a sense of belief ignites amongst its people. For years, Tata Sons has sustained the faith of its consumers because of the legacy of philanthropy that is regularly associated with them.

Corporate social responsibility is the unspoken accountability of every business to its people. It is important to imbibe such values in your culture and take a stance on issues of social relevance. Ensuring generosity and having relations built purely out of goodwill goes a long way in fortifying the eminence of the business.

CONTINUOUS ENGAGEMENT

It is also worth noting that with the dawn of the digital age, looking after brand reputation is even more critical. As the channel of communication remains wide open at all times on social platforms, preserving the integrity of the brand becomes challenging. Begin with taking ownership of the business on social media platforms and engage constantly, especially during times of crisis. Engagement across stakeholders is key.

My own observations find that great brands are built on great reputations. In order to sustain that, there always should be a strategy in place to tackle any curveballs, well-ahead of the imbroglios.

OBSESSING FOR PERFECTION

Interview with the Duke of Richmond and Gordon

The Duke of Richmond and Gordon, Owner of the Goodwood Estate

The first Duke of Richmond, the illegitimate son of King Charles II of England, bought the house that grew to become the Goodwood Estate, in 1697. Today's incumbent, Charles Gordon Lennox, the 11th Duke of Richmond & Gordon is a direct descendent. He took over the Chairmanship of the Goodwood Group of Companies in 1994 and has developed the business with an entrepreneurial zeal. He founded two of the most loved motor racing events in the world, the Festival of Speed (1993) and the Goodwood Revival (1998), restoring the Estate's motor racing heritage. Coupled with horseracing, a hotel, an airfield, two golf courses, an organic farm and much more, the business now employs over 700 people and attracts over 750,000 visitors a year. He also continues his photographic career, as Charles March, and his latest exhibition, at the Galleria Cembalo in the Palazzo Borghese in Rome, opened in May 2018.

New recruits at Goodwood are almost all faced by the Duke on their first day at work and briefed on the values of the Estate, because, he says, 'we're driving behaviour out of values. We now review teams on behaviour as much as results, they're incentivised on behaviour'. Much of the appeal of the Goodwood Estate is fast and beautiful cars, bikes, planes and horses and so its four core values are not the dry values we're used to seeing on the walls of global conglomerates:

(1) It's all about 'obsession for perfection' says the Duke, 'quality is easy to say, but hard to deliver consistently. We must be hitting everything, no matter how small'. He says that if someone is dissatisfied with their experience at any of the Estate's events, 'it's a dagger to the heart. I worry all of the time, does that feel right for us? If you're too relaxed about things, the risks are much higher'.

(2) 'The real thing': On authenticity, he says 'we're very lucky, because we have lots of that. Everything we do has to be true, or people will see through it'. And for Goodwood, with over 300 years of history, that means being

> *... quintessentially English. The overall feel of the*
> *place is English, glamourous, with a great sporting*
> *history — there's a depth to it that people want. The*
> *lineage of the place is super important ...*

.

(3) 'Derring-do' means there has to be a 'wow', that
everything has to be different, exciting and special, 'we
can't just tick boxes'. Goodwood must remain a design-
led business, not a profit-led business. 'If we can do it,
then we should do it' he says, 'and we must be creative'.

(4) The fourth core value is 'sheer love of life', which is
aimed squarely at staff,

> *if we don't love it as a team, being here, doing the*
> *job, then it's unlikely our customers will love it. We*
> *do lots of fun stuff to make people smile, I love it*
> *when people notice that.*

'Sometimes', says the Duke, 'we can do small things that
make a big difference'. In the hotel, if they know someone
likes a particular car, there can be a model of that car in the
room. During the Qatar Goodwood Festival, racegoers are
offered free strawberries and cream — that's very unusual to
be given something for nothing. People respond incredibly
positively to that. 'It's often these little things that can make
your reputation - treating people well and trusting them, we
don't put a rope around anything'.

Although major decisions affecting the Estate are now
'more of a committee process', it wasn't always this way. He
believes that sometimes you have 'just got to jump off the edge'
as there's 'a danger in looking at things for too long'. You've
got to make a decision and get on with it. One of his earliest

big decisions was to rebuild the motor racing circuit that had been closed in the 1960s by his grandfather. 'We knew that Goodwood had a great reputation in the 1960s for motorsport but we weren't sure it still existed'. At the first Festival of Speed, in 1993, chaos ensued as 25,000 people arrived instead of the planned-for 2,000. Today over 200,000 people attend every year. Celebrity enthusiasts of the Estate's events have in recent years included Rowan Atkinson, Keanu Reeves, Tom Cruise, Jay Leno, Valentino Rossi and Lewis Hamilton.

'Reputation is public opinion' says the Duke. And as the secret of the business is authenticity, 'key reputational risks would not be being honest or not being authentic'. He adds:

> *we ask ourselves: do we feel OK about doing this,*
> *for instance, does it fit, does it feel right? The way*
> *the estate is run is also important. We have a big*
> *organic farm. Animals have to live in the right way*
> *and eat the right food themselves. The food we*
> *produce has to be outstanding in every level. To*
> *sustain it all we need to maintain reputation,*
> *nationally and globally.*

When asked what gives him the most joy, the Duke says it's

> *seeing the place giving other people pleasure. From*
> *the days in the Eighteenth Century when aristocrats*
> *raced their horses against each other in match races*
> *at Goodwood, the family have very much shared*
> *this quintessentially English experience.*

He adds, 'it's our role now to decide how best to share this in a way that is meaningful in a modern world'.

JAMES BOND

Anthony Horowitz
Author

He is a cold-blooded killer with an unhealthy appetite for
alcohol – drinking half a bottle of spirits a day – and an addic-
tion to cigarettes. His attitude towards women is, to say the
least, highly questionable and he could also be accused of racism
and homophobia. He never goes to the theatre. He doesn't read
fiction. He has no interest in art. He drives an absurdly expen-
sive and environmentally destructive car. He has few friends.

And yet, for all this, James Bond has been admired and
envied since he was created by Ian Fleming on 17 February
1952. By the time of Fleming's death, the novels had sold
over 40 million copies worldwide and of course there have
been the films – 26 of them so far, grossing at least US$10
billion. It has been said that half the world's population has
seen a Bond movie.

We need to separate the films from the books. The films
cleverly adapt themselves for the times in which they're made
and it's not just the technology that's bang up to date. The
latest incarnation, Daniel Craig, is in every way a modern
man. Gone are the double-entendres and the submissive Bond
girls. In Casino Royale, Craig was the one who emerged from
the sea in the fetching white swimwear.

Even so, the entire franchise rests on the original 12 novels
(and two short story collections) written by Fleming and
these are set in stone. Continuation novels by writers like me

may re-interpret the past but actually change nothing. So, the question remains: What is it about Bond that we love? How has he managed to hang on to his reputation ignoring the swirling clouds of political correctness and changing mores? And even though they are a separate entity, the films have still left their mark. How has Bond survived the excruciating puns ('you always were a cunning linguist'), the inane plots and Roger Moore's safari suits?

It's tempting to answer that Bond is a fictitious character and so cannot be trashed by the tabloids or called out by #MeToo. But this is not entirely true. There are plenty of characters from Billy Bunter to Fu Manchu to Lolita who have found themselves removed from the shelves because they have, in one way or another, fallen out with modern times. There are characters created by Enid Blyton I'm not even allowed to name.

No. The first reason why James Bond's reputation remains intact is simply that he is a creation of genius. We may disapprove of some of his habits and, indeed, many of his attitudes but no matter how fierce our criticism ('the nastiest book I have ever read', Paul Johnson famously wrote of Dr No. 'Sex, sadism and snobbery'.) he appeals to something buried deep inside us to the extent that he is part of us.

Kingsley Amis identified him as the true Byronic hero, a Childe Harold of the modern age, wandering through life but unconnected to it, isolated, alone, somehow tragic. Although Bond's obituary was published in 'You Only Live Twice', we know almost nothing about him. The first chapter of Amis's James Bond Dossier is titled 'The Man Who is Only a Silhouette'. At the end of the day, he is a secret agent. The less that is known about someone, the more difficult it is to bring them down.

And in the case of Bond, who would want to? Getting rid of him would also mean getting rid of a whole gallery of some of the greatest villains in literature: Goldfinger, Rosa

Klebb, Oddjob with his lethal bowler hat, Scaramanga with his third nipple. Bond's friends are our friends too. Who can possibly fail to have some sort of affinity with M − as portrayed in the books or played by Bernard Miles and later by Dame Judi Dench? The gadgets, the fast cars, the cocktails and even the girls may be guilty pleasures but they are pleasures all the same. James Bond is not just a character; he is a world − and it's basically a world that's too good to lose.

In this respect, I would compare him to Flashman, the notorious cad and womaniser created by George Macdonald Fraser. Or Hannibal Lector, the psychopathic cannibal in the Thomas Harris novels. Or, in real life, the Great Train Robbers who stole the equivalent of £50m but badly beat up the train driver in the process. We may not like it but the lesson seems to be clear. Your behaviour may be reprehensible and your moral standing extremely dubious − but you'll keep your reputation so long as you're loved.

THE IMPORTANCE OF UNILEVER CEO PAUL POLMAN

Arun Sudhaman

CEO and Editor-in-Chief, The Holmes Report

At a time when brands jostle for a quick ride on the latest social media bandwagon, it is worth remembering that the best companies develop long-lasting reputations based on a credible point of view and a genuine record of action rather than just words. And there are few that can match Unilever's commitment in this regard (Sudhaman, 2016).

Unilever has come to embody the idea that businesses must be about much more than just profit. Capitalism, according to Unilever CEO Paul Polman, can no longer prosper at the expense of society. Indeed, in Polman's eyes, Unilever is a model for a more sustainable and equitable form of business, a company that does well by doing good.

This kind of rhetoric is not difficult to spout. A quick scan of those wonderful corporate 'values' statements reveals the shocking news that no company actually wants to hurt this planet we inhabit. Yet the list of companies that then follow through on these commitments, at the actual expense of profit, is vanishingly small. And Unilever has effectively emerged as their flag-bearer.

Unsurprisingly, given the importance of leadership when setting a course of action, Polman's thinking has come to define Unilever's brands, which now incorporate social purpose as part of their core positioning, alongside a sustainable living plan that is seen as a model of corporate sustainability. It is a stance that has seen Polman decry the quarterly reporting cycle, arguing that such a short-term mindset detracts from the company's longer-term goals.

Polman's role here should not be underplayed. As Ipsos MORI's Global Reputation Centre report (2016) reveals, 'high profile and strong leadership' is the most important factor when it comes to rebounding from a crisis, according to 58% of the 92 communications professionals on the research house's Reputation Council.

That makes intuitive sense. A crisis is the ultimate test for an organisation and any response should place the CEO and leadership team front and centre. However, plenty of research also indicates that CEOs are often distrusted, particularly in Western markets. Ipsos MORI notes for example that only 23% of the British public trust CEOs to tell the truth, lower than the global average of 39%, and far behind developing economies such as China and India (71% and 69%, respectively).

A trusted, visible, CEO can make a critical difference to an organisation's crisis response. But how many CEOs are really willing to go out on a limb like this? Edelman's Trust Barometer research reveals that in more than half the countries surveyed, the general public cannot name a single CEO (2018). As Richard Edelman has repeatedly noted at the World Economic Forum in Davos, business leaders must step up if they hope to address concerns over such issues as income inequality, and marry profit and purpose in line with public expectations.

In many respects, Polman is the poster-child for this movement, and it has helped turn Unilever into the kind of 'conscious business' that, increasingly, becomes more preferred by consumers and employees. Neither is Polman's thinking framed in terms that market analysts cannot understand. The costs of not acting to create a more inclusive and sustainable society, he has argued, are much higher than the costs of action. One particularly stark example: it costs less to feed the hungry than the various penalties that banks have incurred.

Accordingly, Polman believes a long-term view is required and corporate financial targets must reflect this, rather than a short-term focus on quarterly profits (James, 2018). Money, he has said, is a means to an end. The case must be made for environmental and social capital, all of which requires a longer view.

Polman has also noted that without trust in companies, there can be no genuine prosperity. And trust requires transparency. A total of 75% US graduates, he notes, do not want to work for big companies anymore, they have a strong preference to act for the common good.

With all of this in mind, Polman believes a company's communications department can help shape the world. In particular, he points out that brands with a stronger purpose grow twice as fast. Lifebuoy, as an example, helps children reach the age of five, by improving sanitation in emerging markets. Food brands can help solve the problem of nutrition. And Dove can address women's self-esteem.

Other Unilever goals include carbon neutrality by 2030 and ambitious targets to reduce waste. These, says Polman, do not necessarily translate to quarterly earnings guidance. Too much board discussion focuses on shareholders, such as the powerful multibillion-dollar pension funds – a phenomenon that Polman does not necessarily think is healthy.

Instead, Polman wants companies to report their contribution to sustainability goals, and also the purpose of their brands. In this regard, the Global Reporting Initiative is crucial. Moves like these put Unilever at the forefront of efforts to make business more responsible. Yet, as Polman surely knows, unless more big companies – and, indeed, their communications chiefs – follow Unilever's lead, many of these ambitious global goals will prove critically difficult to realise.

THE SECRETS OF BRITAIN'S MOST TRUSTED PERSON

Interview with Martin Lewis

Executive Chair and Founder of Money Saving Expert.

During 2016's acrimonious Brexit referendum, to decide whether Britain should remain in the European Union, a poll showed that Martin Lewis was the person most trusted by the British people to help them decide how to vote (The Spectator, 2018). That shouldn't have been a surprise, as he's often the British man most searched for on Google in the United Kingdom and every week 12 million people (on request) receive his Money Tips email. His business, Money Saving Expert (MSE), began in Martin's living room in 2003 and has grown to become the single most powerful voice in Britain on saving people money and campaigning for financial justice. So much so, that in 2018, his Martin Lewis Money Show was Britain's most-watched current affairs programme.

In a cynical country like Britain, intent on searching for hypocrisy and with a love of bringing people down, being famous for being 'trusted' is like having a target on your back. But Martin has a secret to building his reputation for trustworthiness, 'I'm paranoid' he says, 'no one is as critical of what we do as I am and I constantly go through all of our activities with a cynical eye'. He adds, 'we don't give anyone any reason to attack us. It's simple. If you want to be trusted, be trustworthy, honest and transparent'. You could add obsession as part of his secret, like he says 'there's nobody thinking about what I do, more than I do'.

MSE's clarity is a model for those businesses constantly trying to invent their purpose. Its objective is saving people money and when challenged, 'what about customer service', Martin's reply is 'that's not what I do'. He also scrupulously avoids 'conflict of voice' in his journalism, as he never himself voices a company statement, as he is solely there to speak to and on behalf of consumers. His obsession with transparency sometimes extends to very long articles and investigations and 'showing the working' that supports his recommendations. His rationale is that while 95% of his audience may not care, 4% want to see evidence of process and 1% really do care. He believes that all corporates should think the same way, as it's the 1% who often influence other people's opinions. As he says, 'sometimes it's complicated, but you have to tell people what you're doing and why – and not in a smaller font'.

Studying business for many years as a journalist and campaigner, while simultaneously running a consumer campaigning organisation, has given Martin a highly developed understanding of how business and trustworthiness interreact in major corporations. He recalls being invited to Number 10 Downing Street, home and workplace of the British Prime Minister, David Cameron, together with the Chief Executives of the country's largest energy providers. At the meeting, an energy company leader asked for the Prime Minister's help 'because our customers don't trust us'. Martin explained that people don't trust energy companies because they aren't trustworthy, deliberately confusing customers with complex tariffs and offers, to ensure that most people pay more than they have to for energy.

He now goes further than that and believes that, to many companies, being untrustworthy and behaving badly is a part of the business model, 'a company's job is to make money and sometimes, as with the energy companies or banks, behaving in an untrustworthy manner is a way of achieving that'. It's sometimes more profitable for big companies to rely on apathy, inertia and ignorance and not be trusted, than it would be for them to engage customers and explain options properly. He believes companies effectively have a 'trust slider' which doesn't always have to be at 100%. As he says:

> *lots of companies want to be trusted, but are not willing to pay for it and it would be better if they were at least honest with themselves about this.*

Turning back to MSE, he's concerned with the modern world's obsession with speed and wanting to do things quickly. He believes that consumers sometimes prioritise UX (user experience) over UO (user outcome). He will, therefore, occasionally insist on a more clunky transactional process, if it helps to ensure people get what they need, not what they want. He rationalises that even if people are happy with a more convenient option in the short term, they won't be happy with MSE in the long term if they make the wrong decision. As he says, 'paranoia is a great aid to managing your reputation'.

DOVE AND JOHN LEWIS

Danny Rogers
Author and Editor-in-Chief, PRWeek UK

For me, the idea of a 'reputation management case study' is inherently problematic. Don't get me wrong, I love case studies. That is why I wrote a book of the cases that have most inspired me during my quarter century working in the PR industry.

But these were chosen as campaigns that had successfully achieved a defined goal. Therefore, a 'reputation management campaign' could be viewed as an oxymoron. Reputation is essentially trust and − as someone once said − trust takes a lifetime to build, seconds to break, forever to repair.

In reality, reputation management is a relentless, ongoing enterprise. Even the greatest brands, with decades of excellent PR, could potentially collapse within weeks if they fundamentally breach the trust contract with their various stakeholders.

That said, some corporates and products endure for decades because they are based in values, have a solid and consistent strategy and therefore help build long-term trust with a myriad of stakeholders.

Two great examples spring to mind: one is a global campaign that's been running for more than 15 years, the other a much-loved UK campaign that has been running since 2012.

Dove's 'Campaign for Real Beauty' (CFRB) began in 2003 and, at the time of writing, it continues, albeit lacking some of its early lustre and with a few serious hiccups of late.

Is it a PR campaign? Well yes, it started out with that clas-
sic PR tactic: a survey. The survey of female self-esteem in
America revealed some shocking findings, which were then –
with the help of PR agency Edelman – turned into a powerful earned media campaign.

It then expanded into a brilliant ad campaign, thanks to
Ogilvy, and some innovative digital content.

There was also some crucial reputational management
along the way, such as the fact that Dove's product stablemate
at Unilever – Lynx/Axe – was pursuing a laddish, stereotyp-
ical marketing campaign.

However, since then Unilever has very sensibly applied
similarly purpose-driven campaigns to most of its brands,
including Lynx/Axe, which has re-established the authenticity
at a corporate level.

Dove has doubled its global sales over the period of
CFRB. The campaign has many copycats around the world.
And, the acid test, Unilever is one of the world's most trusted
corporations.

Meanwhile UK retailer John Lewis has also rewritten the
rules on long-term corporate-meets-product campaigning via
its 'thoughtful giving' strategy.

Each year since 2011 in the run-up to Christmas, the
department store group has released an emotional film based
on the values of thoughtful giving, many of which have really
captured the national zeitgeist.

As well as powerful creative featuring cute bears, hares and
penguins, the concept of thoughtful giving has extended into a
number of charity tie-ups such as Age UK and Barnardo's.

Crucially, this strategy is based on the corporate values
of an employee Partnership whose stated purpose is 'the hap-
piness of its members' and 'satisfactory employment within a
successful business'.

So, the authenticity also derives from the campaign's commercial effectiveness, often having achieved double-digit annualised sales growth, which senior management has directly attributed to the campaign.

We see that trust built through consistency and authenticity tends to require less reputation management on a tactical level.

3

THE VALUE OF REPUTATION

An organisation's reputation is hugely valuable. Legendary American investor, Warren Buffet, wrote to his managers, 'We can afford to lose money – even a lot of money. But we can't afford to lose reputation – even a shred of reputation' (Yahoo Finance, 2018).

I don't believe there is any debate over whether reputation is valuable. Ask anyone who has ever advised a CEO and seen their reaction when their reputation or honesty are questioned. Or, more extreme still, seen the reaction of an investment banker or private equity investor on being questioned about their integrity.

The interesting debates are over how and in what ways reputation is valuable. And whether reputation is a tangible or intangible asset.

Writing in the *Harvard Business Review (2007)*, Eccles, Newquist and Shatz estimated that 70–80% of a company's market value comes from 'hard-to-assess intangible assets such as brand equity, intellectual capital, and goodwill'.

The 2018 UK Dividend Report (Reputation Dividend, 2018) calculates that reputation represents 41% of the market value of the 100 largest companies listed on the London

Stock Exchange. The three reputations that contributed the most to value with investors were management quality, financial soundness and a reputation for the efficient use of corporate assets. This emphasises the earlier point that organisations have different reputations for different things with different audiences.

Top of the tree in Reputation Dividend's report was Unilever, with reputation contributing 56% of market value. This highlights the importance of CEO Paul Polman, 'the capitalist with a moral compass', who is praised by Arun Sudhaman on pages 18 to 21 of this book.

A TANGIBLE ASSET

Most discussions of reputation are clear that it is an intangible asset. I get this. But then Coca Cola, Smirnoff and a whole host of Disney characters are also intangible assets that appear on the balance sheet. I'm not convinced that reputation should itself appear on the balance sheet as I can see obvious flaws in this, particularly for organisations such as banks (although I'd be interested in the debate).

I am convinced, however, that reputation should be spoken of as a tangible asset. While it is real and not real at the same time, it exists. You can feel its presence and power. Warren Buffet can buy companies at a slightly lower price than private equity rivals because he has built a reputation as the 'buyer of choice'. Sellers believe that he is invested for the long term and will allow them to run their companies with relative autonomy. This is a tangible benefit.

In May 2018, Britain's upmarket supermarket Waitrose was selling its own brand 'essential' baked beans for 80p/kg while discounting rival Aldi is selling its 'Corale' beans for 68p/kg. The same day Heinz baked beans are selling for between £1.20/kg and £1.93/kg depending on variety. Even allowing for the possibility of better quality ingredients, that's a big, tangible brand, reputation or brand reputation (depending on your choice of terminology) benefit[3].

The bond markets assess investor confidence in Governments' ability to pay back loans. In May 2018, Switzerland and Japan could borrow money and pay almost no interest to investors, Germany had to pay just 0.28% interest, the UK 1.21%, Australia 2.68%, USA 2.86% and Greece 4.57% (*Financial Times*, 2018). Reputation matters – and a poor reputation costs money.

21 OF THE WAYS REPUTATION ADDS VALUE TO AN ORGANISATION (MORE THAN THE CFO THINKS)

Reputation is not only a tangible asset, it affects company performance in many more ways than most appreciate. The diagram on page 32 shows 21 of the benefits of a strong reputation to an average company – and that's definitely more than the average CFO realises. Tangible benefits are felt by every part of a modern organisation (see Diagram 1 on page 32).

Opinium Research surveyed international reputation managers, corporate communicators and public relations professionals in April and May 2018.

To those closest to the reality of reputation, the benefits are obvious. A total of 88% believe that a business with an enhanced reputation can recruit and retain the best staff. A total of 76% believe that stakeholders are more likely to give an organisation with a good reputation the benefit of the doubt. The full table (1) is on page 33.

Of the C-suite, it's the CEO who believes most in the impact of reputation management on the bottom line; a total

Diagram 1. The Benefits of a Strong Reputation.

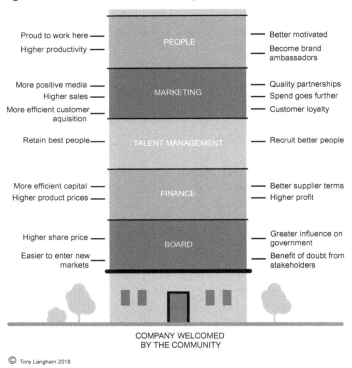

Proud to work here — PEOPLE — Better motivated
Higher productivity — — Become brand ambassadors

More positive media — MARKETING — Quality partnerships
Higher sales — — Spend goes further
More efficient customer aquisition — — Customer loyalty

Retain best people— TALENT MANAGEMENT — Recruit better people

More efficient capital — FINANCE — Better supplier terms
Higher product prices — — Higher profit

Higher share price — BOARD — Greater influence on government
Easier to enter new markets — — Benefit of doubt from stakeholders

COMPANY WELCOMED
BY THE COMMUNITY

© Tony Langham 2018

of 90% reputation management professionals say that the CEO believes (see table on page 34). That's even more than the 81% who say their CMO believes. The most sceptical is the CFO, but even then, the majority say their CFO believes in the value of reputation management.

Table 1. The Benefits of an Enhanced Reputation.

**"Which of the following, if any, do you generally think
of as direct benefits to a business that enjoys an
enhanced reputation?"**   **Total (%)**

Ability to recruit and retain the best staff	88
More positive media coverage	82
Greater likelihood of receiving benefit of the doubt from stakeholders if reputational damage incurred	76
Greater influence on Government	71
Higher quality commercial partnerships	62
More effective marketing/sales activity	62
Higher share price (if a listed business)	50
Higher sales levels	50
Ability to raise capital or borrow money at better rates	45
Negotiation of more favourable terms with suppliers	44
High profitability	39
Higher pricing of products	34
Ability to operate more easily outside the domestic market	33
Improved financial ratios such as return of capital employed, earnings per share	30
More effective/better priced acquisitions	29
Greater celebrity endorsement	25
None of these	1
Don't know	0
Base	112

Base: Opinium Research interviewed 112 senior corporate communications, public relations and reputation management professionals, contacted via the PRCA and ICCO, primarily in Europe, between 20 April and 30 May 2018.

Table 2. Who Values Reputation Management?

"Thinking about your own company/your clients' companies, how much do you think each of these groups believe day-to-day management of corporate reputation affects the organisation's bottom line?"

	% Saying a Reasonable or Large Amount
CEO	90
CMO	81
Board	80
Senior managers	75
CFO	59
Staff in general	49

Base: Opinium Research interviewed 112 senior corporate communications, public relations and reputation management professionals, contacted via the PRCA and ICCO, primarily in Europe, between 20 April and 30 May, 2018.

According to professionals, the most tangible impact of reputation is enabling an organisation to recruit and retain the best people. In a survey conducted for this book, Opinium Research endeavour to put a specific value on this.

ME, NOT YOU: WHAT REPUTATION MEANS TO THE WORKING MAN (OR WOMAN)

Emily Dickinson, James Stevens and James Nicandrou

Opinium Research

More than a quarter of the value of small and mid-sized firms is tied to their reputation.[4] Yet, whilst business owners and managers acknowledge that the perceptions of their customers and prospects has a direct and profound effect on their company's bottom line, the impact of a company's reputation on current and future employees is both less well-recognised, and less understood.

In April 2018, Opinium interviewed 2,006 workers in the UK to uncover exactly what the concept of reputation meant to them, determine the value to their employers and identify how businesses could improve.[5]

SHORT-TERM GAIN, REGARDLESS OF LONG-TERM PAIN

For workers, a company's reputation is not influenced by peripheral corporate values but by short-term, personal experience. When asked to choose which three factors were most important in determining a company's reputation, the top three selected characteristics were: how the company treats their

employees (43%), how they treat their customers (33%) and
the quality of products, goods and services produced (33%).

Intangible attributes traditionally perceived to contribute
positively to a firm's reputation and long-term success with
wider society apparently registered scant or little interest with
employees. Ethical conduct, growth prospects and philanthropic behaviour were only placed by 16%, 6% and 1% of
employees in their top three.

IF YOU LIKE ME, I'LL LIKE YOU BACK

But how much do a worker's perceptions of their company
really matter to the business?

On the face of it, very little.

When asked directly, only 15% of workers said that reputation was one of their top five factors they considered when
deciding where to work. Salary (61%), work/life balance
(54%), location (53%), job security (43%) and interesting
work (41%) were unsurprisingly the factors most highly
rated by potential job seekers. So far, so unremarkable.

Yet, if a candidate must choose between two jobs which
perform equally in terms of these criteria, the employer's
brand — their reputation — can become the determining
factor in both the decision and the conditions of their acceptance. On average, UK workers would be willing to take an
annual pay cut of 5.1% to work for a business with a better
reputation and would require a pay increase of 17.6% to
switch to the same role in a company with a worse reputation. This rises to 18.3% for those earning above the regional
average for their area, but perhaps more significantly, falls by
less than 1% for those with salaries below the threshold. For
millennials, the group feted for taking their ethical values to
the boardroom, the trend continues with these employees

seeking over a 22% increase in pay to move to a company with a worse reputation.

The financial implications of a poor reputation on the business extend to current employees. Of those, who did not feel valued by their current employer, over a third said that they were very likely to change jobs within the next 6−12 months. Reputation, defined by the workers themselves as the treatment of staff, remains a powerful tool for the attracting and retaining talent at below market rates. (Tables 3 and 4).

Table 3. Increased Salary and Reputation.

"What percentage increase of your current salary would persuade you to switch to the same role in a company with a worse reputation?"

		Age		
	Total	18−34	35−54	55+
Under 10%	12%	16%	13%	8%
11−20%	16%	20%	20%	10%
21−30%	9%	15%	10%	6%
Over 31%	19%	22%	18%	18%
N/A − I would not switch to a company with a worse reputation	44%	27%	39%	59%
Average (including those who would not switch company)	17.6%	22.1%	18%	15%

Source: Opinium Research online survey (26−30 April 2018) in the UK of 2,006 working adults aged 18+.

Table 4. Decreased Salary and Reputation.

"What percentage of your salary, if any, would you be willing to sacrifice in order to work for a company with a better reputation?"

	Total	Age		
		18−34	35−54	55+
Under 10%	32%	42%	36%	23%
11−20%	9%	14%	9%	6%
21−30%	3%	3%	2%	3%
Over 31%	2%	2%	3%	2%
N/A − I would not sacrifice any of my salary	54%	39%	50%	67%
Average (including those who would not sacrifice salary)	5.1%	6.3%	5.4%	4.1%

Source: Opinium Research online survey (26−30 April 2018) in the UK of 2,006 working adults aged 18+.

MIND THE GENDER GAP

Women have traditionally been perceived to place greater emphasis on a company's reputation when deciding where to work. This believed behaviour has been lauded as evidence of why full-time female workers in the UK earn an average of 9.1% less per hour than their male counterparts.[6] Of the women polled by Opinium, 59% earned less than their regional average, compared to 37% of men.

Reputation, however, is only slightly less important to women: when selecting an employer 13% rank it in their top five attributes compared to 15% of men, and on average, women would require a 16% pay increase to switch to the same role in a company with a worse reputation, compared to the 19% increase demanded by men. The argument that women's low pay is a result of their decision to prioritise working for 'a good company' over financial compensation is rendered void. For reputation, our research shows equal importance to both genders.

SO, WHAT NOW?

Simply put, to improve their reputation, businesses need to recognise and reward the value their employees bring to their company. Failure to change this approach will have not only reputational but financial consequences.

4

MEASURING REPUTATION (AND THE CURRENT STATE OF PLAY)

REPUTATION CAN BE MEASURED

Every aspect of every element that constitutes reputation can be measured.

Reputation is what key audiences think and feel about a person, organisation or Government – 'perceptions not facts' – and perceptions can easily be measured. The Reputation Institute estimates that most organisations have an average of eight key audiences that are crucial to their success. These could be: customers, intermediaries or retailers, commentators and experts, media, staff, Government, regulators, suppliers and business partners.

Opinion surveys can measure what these audiences think and feel. There are plenty of other means of assessing what these audiences actually do, from sales figures to legislation passed to levels of staff turnover.

So, it's simple, you might think. Surely every organisation must be commissioning such a reputation audit, producing a quarterly report (or something way more dynamic), structuring a Board level discussion around it and using that discussion to feed, build and monitor a reputation management plan? The answer is that some are, but most are not.

WHY ISN'T EVERYONE DOING IT?

One of the key reasons is that companies still have too many silos and haven't (yet) restructured to reflect the modern world. Customers don't see organisations as silos of marketing, communications, customer service and sales. But many companies still exist in that form. The silos in a business don't want to think holistically as it would mean fewer senior managers. They would prefer to talk about brand as distinct from reputation and customer views in isolation, rather than in the same conversation as employee views.

At the top, there are some organisations and CEOs that prefer to lead on instinct. In these organisations, reputation audits can be sources of inconvenient truths, and are often avoided.

On a more prosaic level, there is also scepticism about the validity and accuracy of different methodologies. Because you do have to choose. Presenting a holistic view of an organisation's reputation across eight or more audiences (possibly mixing opinion research and behaviour) is a complex task. Focusing the Board on something as complex as that carries some risk.

You may think that budget is a constraint, but I don't believe it is. Organisations are almost certainly spending big on data analytics and conventional market research. In any event, agreeing to look at reputation holistically can often save money by reducing duplication across an organisation. The only time that budget is an issue is if one of the old-style silos (like corporate communications) tries to take on the task without the support of other silos (like insight and marketing). Then budget is a key factor.

MEASUREMENT IN FUTURE

As reputation rises higher up the corporate agenda, I'm convinced that the holistic measurement of reputation will become the norm.

My preference is for data that exist in context, which means normative data. By that I mean data that allow comparison with other similar organisations. I'm a fan of organisations like the Reputation Institute and the Ipsos Global Reputation Centre. Both have tried and tested methodologies that enable historic comparisons as well as comparisons with companies across all sectors across the world.

I'm also a fan of impartial industry standards like *Fortune*'s The World's Most Admired Companies research, or the work across the world by The Great Places to Work Institute. These surveys provide insight that often remains unused by companies.

THE CURRENT STATE OF PLAY

The rest of this chapter moves from a theoretical discussion to look at a snapshot of what is happening in the world in 2018. First, Richard Edelman discusses the implications of the 2018 Edelman Trust Barometer in 'The Battle for Truth'.

That's followed by Stephen Hahn-Griffiths, of the Reputation Institute, discussing their 2018 RepTrak on global company reputation and then country reputation. The trends shaping the current reputation environment, highlighted by both organisations are particularly interesting and we will return to discuss the implications of those in Chapter 11.

THE BATTLE FOR TRUTH

Richard Edelman

President and CEO, Edelman

In 2018, we find the world in a new phase in the loss of trust: the unwillingness to believe information, even from those closest to us. The loss of confidence in information channels and sources is the fourth wave of the trust tsunami. The moorings of institutions have already been dangerously undermined by the three previous waves: fear of job loss due to globalisation and automation, the Great Recession, which created a crisis of confidence in traditional authority figures and institutions while undermining the middle class and the effects of massive global migration. Now, in this fourth wave, we have a world without common facts and objective truth, weakening trust even as the global economy recovers.

Gresham's Law, based on the eighteenth century observation that debased currency drives out the good, is now evident in the realm of information, with fake news crowding out real news. Leaders are going directly to the people, bashing the media as inaccurate and biased. These forces are taking a toll. According to the 2018 Edelman Trust Barometer, media has become the least-trusted global institution for the first time, with trust scores of over 50% in only six nations, five of which are in the developing world. Putting pressure on trust in media is declining trust in search engines and social media. People have retreated into self-curated information bubbles, where they read only that with which they agree, as if selecting their playlist for music. Half of respondents indicate that they consume mainstream media less than once a week. Nearly six in 10 agree that news organisations are politicised, and nearly one in two agree that they are elitist. Nearly two-thirds agree that the average person cannot distinguish good journalism from falsehoods.

This year also brings a change in the ecosystem of trust, which had become increasingly premised on peer-to-peer discussion. The credibility of 'a person like yourself' declined substantially, and peers are no longer the most-believed source of information. There is renewed confidence in experts, notably technical experts and academics (63% and 61%, respectively), as well as a fast recovering belief in CEOs (up from 37% to 44%), rewarded for speaking out on issues.

At the same time, in the two most powerful nations in the world, China and the US, trust is moving dramatically in opposite directions, with China showing the most extreme positive changes in trust and the US the most extreme negative changes this year.

The US is enduring the worst collapse ever recorded in the history of the Edelman Trust Barometer (Edelman, 2018). This is led by a decline in trust in government, which is down 30 points among the informed public and 14 points among the general population[7], while for the informed public trust in each of the other institutions sank by 20 or more points. General population trust declined nine points on the Trust Index scale to 43, placing the nation in the lower middle segment. But informed public trust imploded, down 23 Trust Index points to 45, ranking the US lowest of the 28 nations surveyed, and all but eliminating the trust gap between the informed public and the mass population. This decline is transversal, across age, region and gender.

China's trust is soaring: it is now the number one nation on the Trust Index among both the informed public and the general population. The government and media have always been highly trusted, but there is an inexorable rise in business and NGOs. The middle class is growing quickly and Chinese brands such as Tencent and Alibaba are moving aggressively into global markets. China's trust scores are nearly matched by India, the UAE, Indonesia and Singapore, while the Western democracies languish mostly in distruster territory, challenging the traditional geo-political vision of satisfaction with systems.

The 'mass-class' divide persists, with only seven nations in the distruster category for the informed public, while among the general population 20 of the 28 nations surveyed now fall into the category of distrust. Declines of trust are no longer linked as closely to economic woes but instead to specific violations, such as quality control falsification at Japan Inc.'s Kobe Steel or the bribery scandals at Brazil's JBS.

The employer is the safe house in global governance, with 72% of respondents saying that they trust their employer to do what is right. By nearly a two-to-one margin, a company is trusted to take specific actions that both increase profits and improve economic and social conditions.

There are new expectations of corporate leaders. Nearly seven in 10 respondents say that building trust is the number one job for CEOs, ahead of high-quality products and services. Nearly two-thirds say they want CEOs to take the lead on policy change instead of waiting for government, which now ranks significantly below business in trust in most markets. This is the time for business to address the wage stagnation of the working class over the past two decades while acknowledging the need to retrain employees who are about to be replaced by automation.

There is a desperate search for the terra firma of stability and truth. The fourth wave of the trust tsunami, the rise of disinformation, is perhaps the most insidious because it undermines the very essence of rational discourse and decision making. Silence is now deeply dangerous — a tax on truth.

The consequences of a loss of belief in reliable information is volatility, societal polarisation and an ebbing of faith in society's governing structures, slowing economic growth and tempting leaders to make short-sighted policy choices. We must heed the warning of the Chinese philosopher Confucius centuries ago: A state cannot survive without the confidence of its people.

This is the existential challenge of our times. Fortunately, we are already seeing the first signs of regret about over-dependence on peers and blind reliance on populist leaders. People's concern about fake news and their willingness to listen to experts show that they yearn for knowledge. The media cannot solve this alone because of economic constraints and the politics of the moment. Every institution must play its part by educating its constituents and joining the public debate, going direct to the end-users for information. That means taking the informed risk to join the battle for truth so that facts triumph over fears.

GLOBAL COMPANY REPUTATION IN 2018: BURSTING OF THE REPUTATION BUBBLE

Stephen Hahn-Griffiths

Chief Reputation Officer, Reputation Institute

Since 2006, prior to the Great Recession, Reputation Institute has been measuring the reputation of leading global companies. Based on the most recent study of global reputation, in January/February of 2018, there is profound evidence that reputation is at the heart of what's driving the world economy. The data indicate that a new era is emerging in which the intangibles of reputation are underscoring political, social and economic changes. Global reputation headwinds and tailwinds related to issues such as the re-emergence of nationalism, the growing importance of female empowerment, corporate tax reform, data privacy and the questioning of fake news, gun control, trade tariffs and beyond are impacting the ways in which companies are viewed. In 2018, the reputation bubble appears to have burst, translating to a decline in reputation of over 1.4 points across all companies globally. This represents the first year of significant reputation decline since the end of the Great Recession (**Table 5** on page 49).

REPUTATION IMPACT ON COMPANIES IN 2018

The bursting of the reputation bubble makes it more difficult for global companies to win and to yield the dividend of

Table 5. Trendline in Global RepTrak 100.

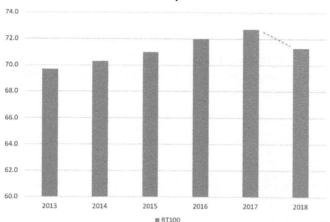

Source: Reputation Institute, average reputation score (out of 100) for companies in the Global RepTrak 100.

economic success. The overall impact on companies suggests an indication of more challenging times ahead, and the likelihood of a more difficult business environment for the short term due to the following observations:

(1) Pressure on market capitalisation and a higher likelihood of trading volatility, due to a −8.1% point decline in willingness to invest

(2) Harder for companies to attract the best talent and become an *employer of choice* — especially for millennials — due to a −6.1% point decline in willingness to work for

(3) Devout loyalty will become more of a rarity, due to a growing lack of differentiation and overall downward trend in purchase intent of −7.9% points

(4) The jury is out for most companies, given the crisis of trust in the court of public opinion, only 38.5% of the world's population trust companies to do the right thing

(5) There is a need to win back trust and increase conviction in always doing the right thing, given that only 30.9% of the informed general public attribute companies with benefit of the doubt

WHAT IT TAKES TO WIN ON REPUTATION: FIVE POINT PLAN

Across the multi-national companies who made it into the Global RepTrak 100[8] in 2018, there are some key learnings on what it takes to earn a good reputation. The rigour of statistical analysis and causal empirical evidence suggests that the most successful companies propelled by the power of reputation tend to have the following five key trends working in their favour:

(1) *Focus on product and enterprise*
The most important global dimensions in driving reputation are associated with perceptions of products/ services, governance and citizenship. Because of this, the companies that make the link between high-quality consumption experiences with the values and ethics of their corporate brand/enterprise do better.

(2) *Be purposefully genuine*
Purpose-driven companies that are underscored by depth of brand strength, heritage and a deeper sense of emotional connection earn a stronger reputation. Through being viewed as authentic and genuine, and effectively communicating with a sense of openness and sincerity, companies can yield competitive advantage.

(3) *Overcoming messaging white noise*
   Given the sheer volume of daily content created and the
   24/7, 365-days-a-year media news cycle, it's harder for
   companies to get their message to effectively break
   through and manage their corporate narrative. Social
   media can make a significant difference and yield
   reputation lift when it is highly targeted to engage global
   influencers who can generate a major impact.

(4) *Identify with millennials*
   Global companies that generate strong levels of support
   among millennials (especially individuals between 20 and
   34 years of age) outperform the competition. Those
   companies that also have a strong sense of identity and
   emotional connection among millennial women are even
   more successful in driving and inspiring human
   behaviour.

(5) *Unleash a new voice of leadership*
   Companies that are shaped by CEOs who think beyond
   profit and who align themselves with societal
   contribution and highly ethical behaviour do better. A
   more vocal company CEO who creates a narrative as a
   CEO activist can have a significant positive impact on
   reputation and can uniquely set the corporate brand
   apart, being viewed as more ethical, relevant and
   empathetic.

GLOBAL REPTRAK 2018: TOP 10 COMPANIES

Despite the overall global reputation decline, the rankings of
the top 10 companies in 2018 remain relatively stable. As can
be seen from **Table 6**, Rolex is the most reputable company
in the world. This is the third year in a row that Rolex has
topped the rankings, due to its timeless commitment to

Table 6. Global RepTrak 2018: Top 10 Most Reputable Companies in the World.

Rank	Home	2018	Score	
1	Switzerland	Rolex	79.3	
2	Denmark	Lego	77.9	
3	United States	Google	77.7	⬆
4	Japan	Canon	77.4	
5	United States	The Walt Disney Company	77.4	⬇
6	Japan	Sony	77.3	⬆
7	Germany	Adidas	76.6	⬆
8	Germany	Bosch	76.4	⬇
9	Germany	BMW Group	76.1	⬆
10	United States	Microsoft	75.8	⬆

Source: Reputation Institute.

product quality, innovation and sustainability. Only three of the most reputable companies are from the US and three from Germany — the other four are from Japan (two), Switzerland and Denmark.

In terms of rankings movement year-on-year, two new companies made it into the top 10: BMW Group and Microsoft. Google jumped two places from last year and Walt Disney dropped two places. By contrast, Intel and Rolls-Royce are two companies that fell out of the top 10 as compared to 2017 (**Table 6**).

COUNTRY REPUTATION: DEFINING THE CULTURAL APPEAL OF A NATION

It has been an eventful 24 months to say the least.

The emergence of the reputation economy has gathered pace, and the profound effects are increasingly leaving a mark on the world. From the impact of Brexit, the new

Trump administration in the US, the re-emerging might of Russia, nuclear threat of North Korea and 'operation car-wash' corruption scandal in Latin America, there is growing evidence illustrating how the dynamics of reputation are shaping world events.

But the underlying feelings of geo-political tension, grow-ing nationalism and social unrest are not only impacting the reputation of companies – they are also driving the repu-tation of individual countries and the leading world economies.

In 2018, all this has translated into a cloud of growing cultural uncertainty in the world. Based on the most recent Country RepTrak[9]2 study, this uncertainty trans-lates into a year-on-year decline in the overall reputation of the leading countries of the world by more than -1.0 pulse points (the measure of reputation). This in turn, means a universal decline in support across the countries measured of -3.0% points.

The Country RepTrak study fielded by the Reputation Institute and uniquely based on the opinions among the citi-zens of the G8 economies – namely US, Canada, France, Germany, Italy, UK, Russia and Japan – suggests that the world order of country reputation is in flux.

WHAT IT TAKES TO INCREASE A COUNTRY'S REPUTATION

According to the Country RepTrak model, the strong reputa-tion of a country is shaped by a deep sense of emotional con-nection that individuals feel about any given country. These feelings are strongly associated with measures of esteem, admiration and trust and informed by how individuals think about the country based on a combination of rational factors.

Diagram 2. Country RepTrak Dimensions and Attributes.

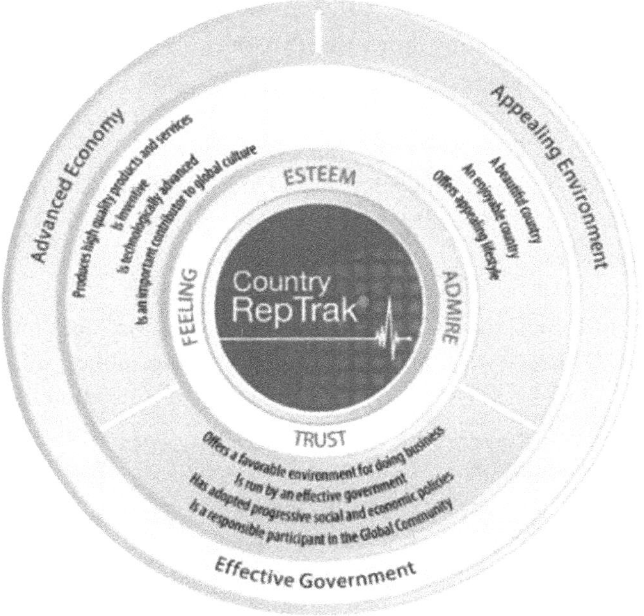

Source: Reputation Institute.

At a macro level, there are three-dimensions that explain how people universally think about the reputation of a country:

(1) Advanced Economy

(2) Appealing Environment

(3) Effective Government

But at a more discrete level, these dimensions are defined by a combination of country-related attributes, that cognitively 'add-up' in the mind's-eye of the citizens of the world to characterise the reputation of any given country (Diagram 2).

KEY TRENDS IN COUNTRY REPUTATION

The shroud of certainty and intangibles that impact reputation makes it more challenging for any given country to win in an ever more competitive global economy. Whether a country is looking to leverage reputation as the means to the end to increase tourism, attract more foreign investment or lure the best minds to study there, there are key actions a country can take to improve their situation:

(1) *Create a Feel-Good Factor*
A total of 51% of the weight of reputation is grounded on the measures of 'feel good' that disproportionately impact the perceptions of a country. Countries that are viewed as welcoming, safe, beautiful and highly principled are associated with an altruistic allure that makes them especially appealing. Perceptions of ineffective government detract from the sense of feel good.

(2) *Size is Not the Biggest Thing*
When it comes to country reputation, the size of population and extent of geographic mass are not major factors in driving consideration. Similarly, the measure of GDP as a KPI of economic might is also not a major factor. This suggests that bragging rights related to size are not at the top of the list of messages when trying to enhance a country reputation. But while big is not always best, it should not be considered as unimportant.

(3) *Being Known and Understood Matters*
Country reputation can be enhanced by depth of familiarity and understanding. In one aspect, the degree of populism as an associated measure of familiarity can enhance reputation, in the degree to which the more

people know you the greater your potential to garner higher levels of support. But familiarity by itself does not guarantee strength of reputation. The strongest association between familiarity and reputation exists when there is also depth of understanding.

(4) *Country Narrative is Key*
Countries with the strongest reputation are those defined by a unique story. Beyond top-of-mind perceptions of country-brand, those nations that have a rich communications narrative in defining their cultural context and human story, have a better reputation. What's interesting is that this country narrative is strongly defined by comments in the news media and on social networks. In other words, a country's reputation is strongly influenced by the narrative of what other people say about it.

COUNTRY REPTRAK 2018: TOP 10 COUNTRIES

Among the top 10 countries overall in 2018 versus 2017, there has been some significant movement in the rankings. As per Table 7, Sweden has now emerged as the most reputable country in the world, with Finland and Switzerland close behind. In the past year, Sweden's reputation has benefitted from the afterglow of its widely reported immigration policies in dealing with Syrian refugees, and an active engagement in gender equality issues in the wake of the #MeToo movement. Finland was buoyed by 100 years of independence celebrations and legalisation of same-sex marriage.

Canada, which was the most reputable country in 2017 has fallen to seventh place following an overall decline in approval of the Trudeau government and fall in perceptions of effective government. Ireland dropped out from the top 10

Table 7. Country RepTrak 2018: Most Reputable Countries in the World.

Rank	Country	Score	
1	Sweden	81.7	Excellent
2	Finland	81.6	
3	Switzerland	81.3	
4	Norway	81.1	
5	New Zealand	79.7	Strong
6	Australia	79.6	
7	Canada	79.2	
8	Japan	77.7	
9	Denmark	76.7	
10	Netherlands	76.1	

Source: Reputation Institute.

in 2018 and was replaced by Japan in the top echelon (**Figure 4**).

Among other countries of note not in the top 10, the UK improved slightly in the rakings moving up to 16th, the US came off an all-time low in 2017 to recover to 34th place, as China also moved up to 45th. However, by contrast Russia fell closer to the bottom of the reputation league of nations to 52nd place.

Interestingly, only four countries among the 55 measured earn the accolade of an excellent reputation, indicating how difficult it is to achieve global recognition. A total of 6 of the top 10 countries were from Europe with strong representation from the Nordic nations, but there were no countries from Latin America at the top of the rankings.

All of the top 10 countries measured had an average familiarity level at around or significantly above the 50% threshold.

5

MANAGING REPUTATION

WE'RE ALL MANAGING REPUTATION

I'm always surprised to hear some practitioners and academics argue that reputation cannot be managed. The argument runs that because reputation is about performance and behaviour – and it's owned by others – it can't be managed. A leading journalist once said to me that 'those with the best reputations, DON'T manage them'. I don't agree. Leaders shouldn't 'obsess' about their reputation, as David Waller points out in the Chapter 6, but they should think about their reputation and by thinking about reputation, they are managing it.

Everyone is managing their own reputation and is part of managing their organisation's reputation, their family's reputation and their country's reputation. It's just that some people are managing reputation well and some badly, others are managing it consciously and some subconsciously.

That's because how we do what we do, is part of doing it. How LEGO makes toys impacts its reputation. What materials it uses and how these are mined or manufactured matters. As does, what it pays its workforce and how it treats them. And whether and where it pays its taxes. And what kind of models it uses to promote its toys. And what packaging it uses. It is no longer enough, if it ever was, to simply make the best toys in the world. It's also how you do it.

Therefore, by 'doing what you do best' or 'being yourself' you are managing your reputation, whether you like it or not. So, it makes sense to accept it and manage reputation consciously.

WHAT IS REPUTATION MANAGEMENT?

Reputation management is the conscious, holistic, integrated, planned, thought through, dynamic, agile and continuous process of managing reputation. It relies on commitment from the top of an organisation and must involve: measurement and analysis; a plan — and coordinated actions to deliver the plan. It involves what organisations do, how they behave and how they communicate.

'How an organisation behaves' can be called its culture, and has been summed up as 'doing the right thing' or 'doing no evil'. My favourite description is IMF Chief Christine Lagarde saying that 'what is needed is a culture that induces bankers to do the right thing, even if no one is watching' (Donnan and Fleming, 2015). The perfect culture is probably one where everyone does the right thing, *particularly* when no one is watching.

And it's the outside world that defines 'doing the right thing' and 'evil'. What was acceptable in the 1970s or even in 2010, may not be acceptable today. What is acceptable in Russia may not be acceptable next door in Finland. And as modern society's expectations grow every year, so do the behavioural standards required of Governments, organisations and businesses.

This explains why the fastest growing area of the PR industry revolves around culture and employee engagement. It's why almost every organisation in the world is striving to define its purpose, its reason for existing, as discussed in Chapter 1. This 'purpose' then has to be explained, turned into mission, vision, values and the whole workforce has to understand how they create the organisation's reputation and how fundamentally important they are to the organisation's success. A great modern business that wants to have a great reputation has to be great at what it does and everyone has to do the right thing when no one is watching.

In Chapter 8, we will discuss the 'reputation management toolkit' and everything that needs to be planned and considered to deliver reputation management. In the rest of this chapter, I'll discuss some of the key current issues.

WHERE ARE THE BIG REPUTATION MANAGEMENT DECISIONS TAKEN?

Although I believe that the Board of a company holds the ultimate responsibility for reputation management as outlined below, that's not necessarily where the big decisions are taken. In an excellent *Harvard Business Review* article on decision making, Bob Frisch argues that in most companies the really big decisions are taken by an informal, flexible and ad-hoc group of two or three people selected by the CEO (2011).

Reputation management decisions are taken every day, by everybody throughout an organisation.

But reputation management is far broader than this. In this book, several people mention the reputational problems at United Airlines in 2017, caused by the video of a passenger, who had paid for his ticket, being forcibly dragged from the plane, subsequently going viral. As John Doorley discusses in the next chapter, the key decision was not that of the security staff dragging the passenger off the plane. They were following company policy. The key decision was taken by the group who decided the policy that certain passengers would be forcibly removed in certain circumstances. They may not have known they were taking a key reputation management decision, but they were.

This is the heart of reputation management. Reputation management decisions are taken every day, by everybody throughout an organisation.

WHY CEOS MAKE THE BEST REPUTATION MANAGERS

Reputation management is not as much about PR or corporate communications as it is about behaviour, but it does include both of those functions. So, who is ultimately responsible for managing reputation?

In a conventional company, the Board is clearly responsible, as reputation is so valuable to the organisation. The CEO has responsibility for delivery and the Chair oversees her on behalf of the owners. For an actor, is Nicole Kidman responsible for her reputation, or is it her agent or publicist? It's clearly her. For a government, it's the President.

In a company, the Board has responsibility for the decisions that determine behaviour. These include the business model and the remuneration and incentivisation policy and the culture. Inclusive, listening cultures have to start with the top, even if they only work if everyone is involved.

In my experience, CEOs often make the best reputation managers anyway. They have the broadest vision, the conviction to act, the desire to take responsibility and the power. But they clearly can't implement and manage the whole programme. That should be the job of the Chief Reputation Officer.

WHERE IS THE CHIEF REPUTATION OFFICER? (AND THE DELAYED EVOLUTION OF PR)

This is a rhetorical question. There are (virtually) no Chief Reputation Officers. But there will be lots, one day. The reasons there aren't now, lie partly in the debate over whether reputation can or can't be managed. However, the main impediment is the siloed nature of most organisations. As highlighted in the Chapter 4, most organisations haven't yet restructured to reflect the modern world and neither has the consultancy sector that serves them. It's hard to say which is the chicken and which is the egg, but it's a good time to discuss the delayed evolution of PR.

Governments, organisations and companies want two things from marketing services: profitable revenue and a strong reputation. To meet this challenge, what was once the relatively homogenous practice of PR is splitting in two (see diagram 3 on page 64).

At one extreme, former PR practitioners and consultancies are heavily focused on marrying creativity with digital know-how and have become 'integrated marketers'. They are indivisible from former advertising and direct marketing specialists, who have become more 'PR-like'. Very soon, the old labels will have disappeared totally and there will just be 'marketing' — unless it will ultimately be called something else.

At the other extreme of former PR, where this book is focused, things are less clear. Here, leading practitioners are

Diagram 3. The Evolution of Marketing Services.

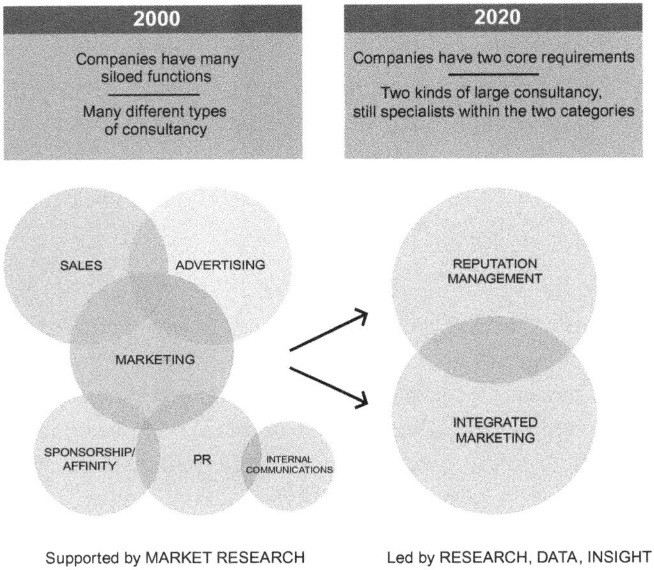

2000	2020
Companies have many siloed functions	Companies have two core requirements
Many different types of consultancy	Two kinds of large consultancy, still specialists within the two categories

SALES   ADVERTISING

MARKETING

SPONSORSHIP/ AFFINITY   PR   INTERNAL COMMUNICATIONS

REPUTATION MANAGEMENT

INTEGRATED MARKETING

Supported by MARKET RESEARCH   Led by RESEARCH, DATA, INSIGHT

© Tony Langham 2018

focused on the key decision makers in the Boardroom and Government and describe their role as strategic, corporate or financial communications; or public affairs or PR. These roles miss the big picture. Decision makers want counsel on how to build, maintain and protect the strongest reputation they can possibly have. In future, these disciplines of strategic, corporate and financial communications and public affairs and PR will be absorbed within the more integral function of reputation management. That's why this book is called, *Reputation Management: The Future of Public Relations and*

Corporate Communications. But in 2018, this new world still seems some way off.

WHY DO ORGANISATIONS ONLY ADOPT THE RIGHT STRUCTURE IN TIMES OF CRISIS?

The new world of reputation management and the Chief Reputation Officer seems a long way off, except when there's a crisis. To Boards and CEOs, the downside risks of poor crisis management far outweigh the upside potential of reputation management in normal business life. So, in a crisis, organisations insist on the most efficient structure to get the job done.

This means getting rid of all silos and building cross-organisation response teams to handle the crisis. Gone are the silos of HR, corporate communications, marketing and customer service — during the crisis they are replaced by small, efficient, fast-acting, cross-company decision-making teams. This invariably works. The popular Machiavellian saying, often referred to by the late Winston Churchill, advised: 'never waste the opportunity offered by a good crisis'. But in terms of post-crisis reputation management, the opportunity to restructure the business is frequently wasted.

HOW CCOs CAN EARN A SEAT AT THE TOP TABLE

The closest role in today's world to Chief Reputation Officer is the Chief Communications Officer (CCO). The constant cry from CCOs (and consultancy chiefs for that matter) is for a seat at the top table. They want to be in the room where it happens. But in the current world, that's not a given.

To be a reputation manager, you have to frequently influence what your organisation does not just how and what it communicates. Many CCOs do not do this.

Furthermore, if the CEO is the ultimate holder of reputation management responsibility (and often the Head of HR or Chief Marketing Officer (CMO) holds the implementation responsibility) then the CCO is not automatically required at the Board discussion. The CCO is currently there when the CEO judges they have something to add to the discussion. This could be because their network is superior to the rest of the C-suite or because they can act as the 'conscience of the company' or the 'voice of society'.

The long-term answer is to become more useful, to become the master of the insight that explains the organisation's reputation and the coordinator of the plan that delivers a better reputation. In short, to transform into the Chief Reputation Officer before someone else does.

UNFAIR ADVANTAGE HAPPENS ALL OF THE TIME

In November 2011, the British city of Leeds came to a halt as celebrity DJ Sir Jimmy Savile received a huge celebrity-packed civic funeral (BBC, 2011). At his death in October, prominent British politician Charles Kennedy had praised Savile for his 'decades of diligence and decency' as did a host of other national figures (BBC, 2011). Within a year of his death, Jimmy Savile was exposed as a serial child and sexual abuser. He's now known to be one of Britain's worst ever abusers with upwards of 450 victims (Brown, 2013). But he made it to the end of his 84-year life with his national reputation intact.

We would all like to believe that the best companies and the best people have the best reputation. And in the long run, they mostly do. But as Jimmy Savile demonstrates (and he was actively managing his reputation) the 'short term' can last quite a long time.

I believe that all of us see unfair reputational advantage around us. In fact, by definition, that's the reputation manager's typical brief, as the average company wants a better reputation than they deserve.

The answer, for the best companies, is to ensure that they're as good at reputation management as they are at everything else. Lesser companies will copy their best lines. Bad people and poor companies will also try to manage their reputation. But in the end authenticity will triumph, as long as relations with the outside world are handled impeccably.

THE REAL REPUTATION MANAGEMENT HEROES

This book appears to revolve around those people that work in Head Office. The CEO, Chair, CFO, CCO, etc. And that's the world I and possibly most of you, work in. But we shouldn't for a second forget the real reputation heroes. Looking at the RepTrak top 10 companies, it's the people that work in factories for Rolex, LEGO, Canon, Sony, Adidas, Bosch and BMW. It's the people that write Google's algorithms, work in Amazon's warehouses and write Microsoft's programmes. They are the real reputation management heroes. Without their work, there would be nothing for Head Office to manage.

6

PERSPECTIVES ON REPUTATION MANAGEMENT

This is one of my favourite chapters in the book. It presents seven hugely varied perspectives on reputation and managing reputation, from leaders in their various fields.

One of the real privileges in putting together this book has been speaking with John Doorley, a pioneer and evangelist, who I've come to see as the father of reputation management. John's book, co-authored with Helio Fred Garcia, *Reputation Management – The Key to Successful Public Relations* was first published in 2006, with the fourth edition due in 2019. It is the best in the field. His essay for this book looks back on the progress of reputation management as a concept, over the last twelve years. He concludes that

> *organisations that are living up to what they say they stand for have the best chance of protecting and optimising the reputation asset. The corollary of that is also true.*

Psychologist Dr Helena Boschi writes about the brain. Helena has worked with my company Lansons to build an exciting 'neurocomms' offering for our clients, and I was delighted that she agreed to write an essay for this book. She argues very persuasively that we have to get it wrong to get it right and that our brain can do it ... if we help it.

I was lucky to secure an interview with two of the power houses of the world of acting, Lindy King and Dallas Smith of United Agents. They discuss 'Movie Actors and Reputation' in a fascinating and insightful interview.

One of the recent books that has made us think about reputation in a more considered way is *Reputation Games* (2017) by Finsbury Co-founder Rupert Younger and FTI Senior Managing Director David Waller. David's essay here looks back at the reputational crises of 2017 and 2018 and concludes that 'if you obsess over your reputation, you are looking at things from the wrong end of the telescope'.

Fu Jing, Managing Director of the Beijing-based China Watch Institute, looks at China's international reputation. He discusses China's need and desire for greater international understanding and a better reputation. He notes that, this can be at odds with Confucian teaching that the superior man should succeed in his actions, but be modest in speech.

Winfried Engelbrecht-Besges, CEO of the Hong Kong Jockey Club writes about 'Reputation, Integrity and Sport'. He says that challenges to the integrity of sport are more complex than ever before. Winfried details the six elements that comprise the Club's 'uncompromising, and holistic approach to integrity assurance'.

And finally, Lansons Consultant Lara Thomas writes 'Opportunity or Risk: A Millenial's Perspective'. She says that 'for the millennial in reputation management, challenging clients and colleagues (with confidence) and holding them to account is commonplace'. One of her doubts about the future is 'the legacy of previous generations of PR professionals' which 'threaten to undermine the strategic value of reputation management'.

I hope you find the seven contributions as stimulating and thought-provoking as I did.

TO MANAGE REPUTATION IS TO TREAT IT AS AN ASSET: NOT TO DO SO IS TO MAKE IT A LIABILITY

John Doorley

Associate Professor, School of Communications, Elon University, USA

I first started thinking about reputation management as a formal discipline when I was head of corporate communications at Merck during the last 12 years of the last century. Then the largest healthcare company and one of the world's most admired companies, its market capitalisation was in the top five of US companies and in the top 10 worldwide. Yet its revenues and tangible assets were a fraction of those of other large market-cap companies.

Some reputation scholars back then wrote that the difference, averaged over time, between a company's market cap and the liquidation value of its assets is reputational capital. A quick, qualitative survey of CFOs indicated they believed that equation overstated the value of reputation. However, the CFOs also agreed the value of reputation was a significant part of the difference. It seemed plausible that, indeed, reputation could be a company's 'most important asset', as CEOs often called it. But executives and scholars thought of reputation as intangible, so they scoffed at the term reputation management.

That's when I designed a process called 'Comprehensive Reputation Management', and copyrighted it with the US Library of Congress in 2003. It defined reputation as the sum of perceptions of the stakeholder groups and was based on the proposition that to manage the parts is to manage the whole. 'Comprehensive Reputation Management' included this formula:

$$R(\text{reputation}) = P(\text{performance}) + B(\text{behaviour}) + C(\text{communication})$$

I included it in the first edition of *'Reputation Management'* released by the scholarly publisher Routledge, Taylor & Francis in 2006. In the second edition, I expanded the formula to include the authenticity factor (Af), a measure of how true the organisation is to its intrinsic identity (what it stands for). If the organisation stays true to what it stands for, it is whole and the Af is one: The sum of performance, behaviour and communication – reputation – is undiminished.

$$R = (P + B + C) \times Af$$

Many communication agencies and even the big consultancies now list 'reputation management' among their practice areas. The fact is that most of them stop at measuring and monitoring reputation, far short of managing it. Most large corporations have risk managers but they usually manage financial and legal risks, with little or no focus on reputational risks, let alone on the upside, the undervalued 'attributes' of reputation.

On the other hand, The Edelman Trust Barometer (Edelman, 2018), which measures that ultimate of benefits of a good reputation, was conducted and published for years before it included drivers of trust similar to the drivers of reputation. The Trust Barometer evolved and is helping lead the field.

Fast forward to 2018, when Routledge is now working with co-author Helio Fred Garcia and me to produce the fourth edition of *Reputation Management*. Reputation managers can reflect on these accomplishments and principles. **This is the good news.**

(1) Studies have shown that the intuitive assumption about reputation is true. That is, companies with better reputations attract more and better job applicants, gain more favourable earned media, have larger premiums, and pay less for goods and services. The most important long-term benefit is trust. Trust is not reputation but rather flows from it.

(2) Studies by Simon Cole (Reputation Dividend, 2018) and others have shown that the value of reputation is approximately 20 % of the market cap of large companies.

(3) More scholars are studying reputation.

(4) More young communicators have gained exposure to the concept that reputation has tangible and significant value.

(5) Reputation surveys teach us a lot. One of the oldest, the *Fortune* Most Admired Companies survey (*Fortune*, 2018) measures the perceptions of three well-informed stakeholder groups, the same as when it began in 1993, using the same eight attributes plus global competitiveness.

A 2014 survey of 1,000 CEO-level executives by The Conference Board (The 2014 CEO Challenge) listed brand and reputation management among their top five strategic priorities, alongside financial soundness, global competitiveness, innovation and human capital. Brand (how the organisation wants itself, a product or service to be perceived) is routinely managed based on brand perception studies which are, essentially, reputation studies with one stakeholder group (customers and prospective customers). So why is reputation, across the spectrum of stakeholders, still not being managed in most companies or organisations?

It is often confused with crisis management. I recently asked five leading communication professionals whether the infamous United Airlines crisis, where a passenger was dragged from the plane belly up, was caused by a failure in reputation management or crisis management. Three answered crisis management. Yet, clearly, the real failure was in not flagging the company policy that required airline employees to contact port authority officers and have a passenger, unwilling to relinquish his seat, removed if the airline needed it. Once the fellow passenger's cell phone register sent, there was nothing the company could do but mitigate the financial and legal damages.

Are some communication professionals failing to see the ethical issue here: the difference between preventing a crisis and waiting for it to happen? Crisis management is big business. Or, might it simply be the case that many communicators, corporate and agency leaders, still fail to see the long-term business advantages and opportunities in reputation management?

Back to the formula: $R = (P + B + C) \times Af$. It leads us, according to those who use it, to these self-evident conclusions and principles:

(1) A failure in performance, behaviour or identity cannot be fixed by communication. If communication did not cause the problem, it cannot fix it.

(2) Reputation management can prevent vulnerabilities from becoming crises.

(3) The process also provides an opportunity to identify attributes where an organisation might be undervalued. For instance, on innovation, executive leadership or employee talent.

(4) The very existence of a reputation management process will identify earlier the looming crisis. That should have been the case at General Motors with the ignition switch crisis and at Volkswagen with the emissions device duplicity. That should have been the case at Michigan State University, USA Gymnastics and The US Olympic Committee, under whose employment and acting with what some victims saw as imprimaturs, Dr Lawrence G. Nasser sexually violated as many as 200 girls and young women. In February 2018, Nasser was sentenced to at least 100 years in prison. (CNN, 2018) The three organisations have denied a cover-up. None can deny a lack of due diligence.

(5) Reputation is the net of favourable and unfavourable perceptions. Therefore, while it is good to think, 'All hands-on deck' when a crisis hits, it is important to resume, with care, pushing out the good news once the fire subsides and good publicity seems appropriate.

(6) The definition of apologies is 'to express regret for something that one has done wrong' (Oxford Living Dictionary). Apologising, even when the individual or organisation did nothing wrong — despite what some

crisis communicators advise – may stop the bleeding, but it is untruthful and bad behaviour. It will, therefore, harm reputation over the long term.

(7) Preliminary studies indicate that companies and other organisations with some formal reputation management structure in place have better reputations.

Finally, the formula will reveal some of the future. Performance will wax and wane, and behaviour will slip, but organisations that are living up to what they say they stand for, have the best chance of protecting and optimising the reputation asset. The corollary of that is also true.

GETTING IT WRONG TO GET IT RIGHT: A CHALLENGE FOR OUR BRAIN

Dr Helena Boschi
Psychologist

A good reputation takes time to build. It requires patience, hard work and consistent behaviour. Reputation can also be destroyed in a moment.

Any reputation – be it personal or corporate – is the aggregate result of many different moments and actions by humans – and nothing tests humans and their reputations more than adversity. The better and bigger the reputation, the more the world watches to see how setbacks are addressed to recalibrate and repair opinion, in order to regain public trust.

Herein lies the problem: the bigger the ego (and often the greater the expertise), the more reluctant we are to admit wrongdoing, no matter how minor. And the instrument responsible for this reluctance is our brain.

Our brain's primary focus is to protect us and keep us alive. It is uncomfortable with uncertainty and it relies on its set of stored beliefs to interpret and regulate its responses to incoming information. When these beliefs are thrown into question by a new piece of information our brain becomes anxious. This mental discomfort is known as *cognitive dissonance*, a term coined by Leon Festinger in 1957 to describe the tension created in the brain when an existing belief is confronted by conflicting information.

A good example of this may be seen in smokers who continue to smoke despite a myriad of associated health warnings. Smokers will often find ways of justifying their continued smoking in various ways so that they can accept it in themselves. In a sense, cognitive dissonance represents a form of psychological armour.

Cognitive dissonance explains why we often cannot admit to being wrong or to feeling chastened by a mistake we have made. Our brain would rather work harder to rationalise or discount any evidence, however compelling, that poses a threat to our existing beliefs, than find ways to change these beliefs or related behaviours. *('I can give up smoking any time'; 'I have relatives in their 90s who still smoke'; 'I only smoke five cigarettes a day').*

The more an ego or identity is tied to a belief *('I am a senior manager with an impressive track record'; 'I am a successful surgeon who has saved hundreds of lives'; 'I am a lawyer who has won numerous cases'),* the more cognitive dissonance will prevent us from accepting any blame or feeling any shame. It makes us blind to our own accountability.

Having a healthy ego is critical to our survival and sense of self-worth. We would not want to be operated on by a surgeon racked with self-doubt. But an ego that is too big can be damaging to the self and the environment in which it operates, often leading to cover-ups and denial. And we hate feeling deceived by others.

History is peppered with examples of strong and successful individuals appearing unable or unwilling to acknowledge their part in a financial loss or an adverse medical outcome for example. Despite leadership pundits pointing to the need to 'embrace failure' and 'fail fast', the fear of reputational damage, together with the ominous cloud of litigation, joins forces with ego to validate and vindicate what we have done. Once we have savoured the sweet fruits of success, it becomes even harder to swallow the shame pill.

Pope famously said, 'To err is human'. Indeed, human civilisation has been built on trial and error. It is what we do about our mistakes that counts, and this is more important than trying to ignore, discount or excuse the fact that these mistakes exist in the first place. Accepting responsibility and learning from what has happened may lead to a better outcome and will certainly strengthen both human and corporate muscle to deal with the future.

Our brain is a wonderful, complex and protective instrument. It is also extremely creative when faced with challenges to overcome. Our beliefs form part of our brain's hardware and they create the necessary reference points and short cuts to help us navigate the vagaries of life. But our beliefs do not form THE truth, they merely represent the world that we have constructed around us. As such they are prone to error, bias and distortion and erroneous beliefs may prevent us from doing what is right. This is a key reason why our brain benefits from a diverse diet of different opinions, experiences and working preferences.

The more we can challenge ourselves and our thinking, the better our capability to form more considered and objective views and modify our behaviour in a spirit of continual adaptation. Nothing builds a reputation better than a story of self-discovery and growth.

Mistakes are an inevitable part of learning and life. A good reputation is forged on honesty and openness, as well as an ability to accept our own human fallibility. Armed with these, we can face the future with a wiser lens.

Our brain can do it, if we help it!

MOVIE ACTORS AND REPUTATION

Interview with Lindy King and Dallas Smith
United Agents

United Agents was formed from the implosion of long-established talent agency PFD in 2007 and in 11 years has grown to become London's premier literary and talent agency. Its roster of actors includes James Corden, Taron Egerton, Ricky Gervais, Kit Harington, Keira Knightley, James McAvoy, Sienna Miller, Rosamund Pike and many more. I spoke to Chair and Co-founder Lindy King (long-term agent for Tom Hardy) and Senior Partner Dallas Smith (long-term agent for Kate Winslet and Eddie Redmayne) at their offices in Soho, London in May 2018.

Debating the success of actors, both agree that it's all about talent. But it is very subjective, as 'four different agents could easily choose four different actors' according to Dallas. Presence matters too. Lindy emphasises the importance of the '30 seconds when an actor walks into a room'. 'Some people have an innate charisma', says Dallas. They agree that unfair advantage can happen in the short term ('a flash in the pan can get you the next one or two jobs' according to Lindy) but ultimately, you build on your reputation.

When we talk about reputation, they're both keen to emphasise the long term, strategic nature of their role. 'You want them to build a career not just get a job', says Lindy. 'With a young actor you're trying to guide them in the choices they make. Trying to establish their reputation as a sought-after property', adds Dallas. Which roles to take, and when, is crucial as 'one bad choice can undermine a reputation' according to Dallas. He added that Eddie Redmayne and Kate Winslet have both made exemplary career decisions throughout. Lindy believes that for example 'you need a body of work first, before you do an action film'. Although she adds that superhero films are more characterful for actors these days, and are wittier and funnier than they once were. However, they are 'only' agents. 'We don't control anything', say Dallas and Lindy.

Both see theatre as a crucial part of building reputation. Dallas believes 'theatre gives an actor great credibility' and to Lindy 'it's a reputation maker, to most actors, stage is their medium'. That's why 'most movie actors have to go back before they're too scared – it always rejuvenates them'. Dallas believes that Eddie Redmayne's initial reputation in the theatre was vital to his long-term success. He adds that 'for the long term, appearing in a good play at the Royal Court (a cutting-edge London West End theatre) is better than accepting a three-year contract to appear in an ongoing

TV series'. The position to get to, according to Lindy, is to build a body of work, then to be able to surprise people, to make people say, 'I never thought they could do that'.

Both are conscious of their own reputations, striving to get casting directors to see their clients ahead of those with rival agencies. 'Our job is to convince casting directors', says Dallas. 'We've tried to acquire a reputation for being a place for rising talent', he says. However, he adds that 'making the agency's reputation has taken a lot of time, particularly our reputation with casting agents'. To convince young actors to join United Agents, he advises them 'to look at the other actors on the agency's roster'. He says, 'I wouldn't take anyone on if it compromised me as a person'.

Dallas and Lindy stress the importance of publicists as they 'help actors retain their reputation – what the opinion makers read is important'. Publicity can be a touchy subject for actors, as Lindy says, 'most actors don't mind publicising their films, but not publicising themselves'. On the subject of social media, Lindy is sceptical: 'some people think that they can promote themselves on social media, but I don't agree, if you're forever on social media, you don't have anything to promote. But most of all, it takes away the mystery and there has to be some mystery'. Though she says, 'I'd let anyone go on Graham Norton (the UK's top chat show host)' as he allows guests to speak and accepts that they, not him, are the stars of the show.

On the issue of #MeToo, Lindy 'hopes it's making a difference and believes there's a solidarity that wasn't there before'.

Rebuilding a reputation or helping an actor have a 'second career' is a key part of the agent's work. Lindy says, 'I use my reputation to say, "trust me, they can do something you've never seen them do"; I'm saying trust me as an agent'.

Both Lindy and Dallas agree that watching the French TV series on Netflix, *Call My Agent,* will give anyone a pretty good idea of the relationship between actor and agent. 'You take risks and sign people you believe in — it's not a science, it's an art', says Dallas. He adds that 'it's an arbitrary business and luck plays such a huge part'. To Lindy, 'you ask them what they're looking for, for their ambition, as you have to know you're the right person'. To Dallas, 'it's an intimate business', while Lindy adds that 'you have to manage the actor's expectations, not crush them'. Asked for their key words, Dallas opts for taste and integrity, Lindy goes for instinct and trust.

REPUTATION GAMES AND WHY IT'S WRONG TO TARGET A GOOD REPUTATION

David Waller

Senior Managing Director, FTI Consulting

The French philosopher Blaise Pascale once posed the following question: 'We do not worry about being respected in towns through which we pass,' he wrote. 'But if we are going to remain in one for a certain time, we do worry. How long does this time have to be?' (Auden and Kronenberger, 1981).

His question goes to the heart of the way that reputations are formed, in personal as well as public and professional life. We care about our reputations if we are part of a community and to be in a community you need to stay in one place long enough to build up the reciprocal ties that bind you into a network.

If you are just passing through, such questions are irrelevant, but if you are staying for a long time, your reputation in that community is extraordinarily important.

There is one major difference between the seventeenth century, when Pascale was writing, and today: our reputations are no long tethered to time and place. The Internet has made a network of the entire world, spanning continents. Reputations are made and destroyed in moments, when in Pascale's day they might have taken a lifetime to build and be extremely difficult to unravel.

Since our book on reputation was published in the autumn of 2017[10], one reputational crisis after another has dominated the headlines. For example, the charity Oxfam has been engulfed by revelations that its staff used prostitutes in Haiti in 2011. As its belated internal investigation made clear, the alleged breaches relate to sexual abuse, exploitation and harassment, nepotism, fraud and negligence.

The movie mogul Harvey Weinstein has been exposed as a serial sex pest and possible rapist, triggering a global backlash against the exploitation and abuse of women by powerful men. The global '#MeToo' campaign has changed the terms of debate: behaviours that might have been swept under the carpet, are now being called out as wholly unacceptable.

The emissions scandal at Volkswagen, Europe's largest car manufacturer is another reputational disaster that runs and runs. VW was exposed as developing and installing technology to get around tests to evaluate how much pollution was emitted by its diesel engines installed in nearly 500,000 cars in the US. The company's brilliant engineering managed to fake good results whenever the cars were tested. When they got back on the road, they went back to emitting as much as 40 times the amount of permitted pollutant.

In the UK, the fall of Toby Young is another example of a reputational collapse, albeit on a different scale. The journalist and champion of free schools was appointed to the board of the Office for Schools with effect from 1 January, 2018. Within a few days, he was out again after details of sexist and offensive tweets made a decade before it became public.

While these crises have different degrees of seriousness, they do have some points in common. The first is that the reputational fallout has been deeply damaging for the institutions and individuals concerned. It will be a brave pundit who would predict that Harvey Weinstein will restore his Hollywood career any time soon. At the time of writing, the pressure on Oxfam is intense; it is fair to ask whether the organisation will survive and in what form, as sponsors, volunteers and celebrities reconsider their commitments to the charity.

This was a key argument of our book: that reputation is more valuable than money in our globally interconnected world. It is not something that you control, but rather it is in the gift of other people – and that's what makes it so powerful. The starting point is your behaviour – what you do. You need to be connected to the right networks, as reputations are created and sustained within networks. And you need to tell a good story about what you are doing, in order for your core competencies to be appreciated.

A second observation about these crises is that individuals and organisations are living in an era of radical transparency: there is nowhere to hide. No doubt Oxfam officials who consorted with prostitutes on Haiti, did so without any expectation that their behaviour would ever become public. But in today's world, the distinction between private and public life is no longer tenable.

Nothing can be hidden: your actions will be caught on a smartphone (think of United Airlines, whose staff were filmed forcibly removing a passenger from a plane, or breaking guitars on the runway) — or a whistle-blower will leak perceived crimes to the press.

And, as Toby Young discovered, an offensive tweet posted online in the middle of the night a decade ago, does not disappear — it will come back to haunt you. In fact, that is true for all of us: our social media record is accessible to employers, customers and colleagues, for all time.

One distinction we draw in the book is between the *character* reputation of an individual or an organisation and *competence* reputation. It is interesting in the case of VW that its core competence as a manufacturer of safe and solid cars, has not been seriously challenged by the disaster and customers still flock to buy their vehicles. However, its character has been tested and found wanting.

In the case of Oxfam, by contrast, a core competence is to have good character — essential for an organisation professing to do good work in the world and relying on the goodwill of volunteers and donors. This sits alongside other, more prosaic competences, like delivering aid projects on time and on budget.

In this treacherous world, where reputational challenges emerge seemingly out of nowhere with such destructive consequences, how should we behave? Should we strive to attain a better reputation?

We argue strongly against targeting a good reputation, except insofar it is a by-product of being good at what you are supposed to do. This applies to individuals as well as organisations: do a fabulous job and your reputation will take care of itself. Obsess over your reputation and you are looking at things from the wrong end of the telescope.

THE LONG MARCH TO BUILD CHINA'S INTERNATIONAL REPUTATION IS JUST BEGINNING

Fu Jing

Managing Director, China Watch Institute

Mianzi, face culture, or intention to gain a good reputation, is deeply rooted in Chinese society. Conversely, we are also taught that to become the superior man, as Confucius put it, we should be modest in speaking, but exceed in our actions.

These traditional cultural elements are reflected in how China is building its international reputation: we care about reputation, but we are not keen on designing communication strategies and using public relations tools and skills.

That is why, on many occasions, when delivering speeches or at seminar debates, Chinese participants are still less confident than Westerners and sometimes Africans, particularly if the working language is English.

2018 is a historic moment as it is the 40th anniversary of reform and the globalisation of China, which will continue to focus on opening the door wider in coming years. China has concentrated on achieving what it wants to achieve in the world, but has only gradually realised the importance of international reputation management and is on a steep learning curve.

Some may ask: if the deep-rooted Chinese culture doesn't care enough about external communication and publicity, why is international reputation management so crucial for China?

To gain international reputation, China needs to be better understood. China wishes to be seen as a prosperous, inclusive, green and innovative economy that could one day equal or even surpass the development levels of the advanced economies.

This ambition has grown since 1978, when China badly needed capital, technology and advanced experience. Even now, China is still hunting for these treasures worldwide and internally. At the same time, Chinese investors, students and tourists have travelled worldwide to do businesses, study or tour, and it would help them if mutual understanding was increased.

Gaining international reputation is not the end in and of itself, but a means to an end. It is a tough mission, as Chinese culture is, somehow, still a barrier.

What's more, English-language content still dominates on the global stage and the Western media still speaks louder than those from the emerging economies. Generally speaking, the outside world has less desire to understand China than China does to understand the rest of the world. Right now, the number of Chinese nationals travelling to see the rest of the world vastly outnumber Western visitors to China.

Furthermore, ideological factors also matter to China even though it is now a market economy. This adds to the challenges China faces in managing its international reputation.

China has been facing these challenges.

During the past decade, since hosting the Olympic Games in 2008, China has become a regular venue for international conferences and events, in many cities outside Beijing. And its leaders have travelled worldwide to speak and communicate. Some observers even say that President Xi Jinping has become the most frequent flyer among the world's leaders, in his attempt to shape international understanding and consensus.

In recent years, many Chinese embassies have expanded their functions from press departments into public diplomacy. And many ambassadors are eloquent, timely, persuasive and assertive in their writings and speeches.

At the same time, Chinese media outlets have started to post more journalists worldwide and some have partnered with publications in other countries. Chinese businesses have increased their global presence realising the importance of fulfilling their corporate social responsibility and deepening bonds with local communities as a result.

Compared with what the West did in the world and in China during previous decades, China has just taken its very first steps in managing its international reputation. The sharp comparison of the many foreign-owned public relations consultancies operating in China with the relatively small number of those Chinese companies working in foreign countries, says a lot.

In the coming years, it is important for Chinese communication and publicity businesses to form partnerships with outside experts. Together they can better advise the Chinese embassies, investors, media and other organisations to do a more professional job in building their reputations, diminishing risks and managing crisis. Many people suggest that 'content is king' in managing reputation. But if we look at who is creating the content most widely used in the media, we rarely see the names of Chinese authors or contributors. It is even rarer to see them taking the lead in drafting reports. Chinese opinion leaders have still not gained the worldwide presence that China's economic might deserves.

That is one of the many examples of the large gap that needs to be closed to enable China to achieve the international reputation it is aiming for.

REPUTATION AND INTEGRITY IN SPORT

Winfried Engelbrecht-Bresges, GBS JP
Chief Executive Officer, The Hong Kong Jockey Club

In any discussion concerning reputation and integrity in sport, the first realisation must be that the former is ineluctably the product of the latter. A sport's reputation is built on the foundation stone of its integrity; the reputation of a sport is intrinsically and inextricably linked to the integrity of that sport. Whilst the concepts of a sport's 'reputation' and 'integrity' are ultimately intangible, it is undeniable that the health and success of a sport is dependent upon them. That no integrity equals no reputation is the simple but ironclad calculus. As noted sports lawyer, Richard McLaren, has observed, once integrity is lost 'it is very difficult to ever retrieve'[11] (2008). It follows that although the reputation of a sport may potentially withstand temporary lapses in its integrity from time to time, the consequences of a complete failure in a sport's integrity are catastrophic, with the permanent destruction of the sport's reputation and sustainability the inevitable outcome. Thoroughbred racing is a sport which has long recognised the existential threat that integrity risks pose and which has a demonstrated history of facing those threats through strong regulation.

The unique qualities of sport have long ensured its special place within society. As IOC President Jacques Rogge has expressed, sport is based on a hierarchy that derives its social and moral values from the concept of merit'[12]. (Boniface and

Lacarriere, 2011) It is the 'concept of merit' that enlivens sport's social and moral values and therefore establishes and drives the sport's reputation. Where merit is determinative, the 'best' wins. However, in order for 'merit' to be fairly and reliably determined, the sporting contest must take place on a 'level playing field'. A level playing field allows each participant the opportunity to win on their merits, in a competition free from the influence of any corrupting factor which may undermine or pollute the uncertainty of the sporting event.

The concept of integrity in sport is multi-dimensional and multi-layered. It covers the notions of the 'level playing field' and fair play, and generally facilitates the 'concept of merit' and sporting excellence. It demands clear and fair rules and regulations, which are respected and upheld by participants and officials alike. However, the concept of integrity in sport also reaches further. Amongst other things, it encompasses the health and welfare of the sport's participants and requires high standards of governance and commercial dealings, by honest and competent administrators.

By focusing on, and maintaining the integrity of sport, governing bodies seek to protect not just the reputation of the sport, but specifically the interests of a sport's stakeholders: the fans who follow it; its participants who depend upon it for their livelihood; and the sponsors who associate themselves with it in exchange for financial support. Without the maintenance of the highest standards of integrity, a sport's reputation flounders and it will wither whilst the stakeholders will be exposed and fall away. As a result, it is critical that robust and uncompromising integrity-related regimes be established, implemented and enforced within sports. A strong regulatory approach merely reflects the importance of maintaining the integrity of sport, and the critical need to protect a sport's reputation and stakeholder's interest.

The sport of racing has a long history of addressing integrity threats, and has long led the sporting world in the fight against doping, amongst other matters. By way of the example, the Hong Kong Jockey Club has developed an uncompromising and holistic approach to integrity assurance which places the integrity of the sport at the core of the Club's function. That approach comprises a diverse, but complementary range of measures and resources, including:

(1) *Rules and Regulations:* strict but fair Rules of Racing, regulations and policies: these underpin the entire integrity regime, and generally regulate the conduct of races and participants;

(2) *Expert and Professional Human Resources*: The Club employs a broad range of highly experienced professionals to perform dedicated and expert functions across all key racing integrity areas. These resources ensure that the Club has highly experienced racing stewards and investigators to review any potential breaches of the Rules and that the Club can cooperate effectively with law enforcement and intelligence bodies;

(3) *A Comprehensive Anti-doping Program and Racing Laboratory:* in order to support the sport's zero tolerance approach to the use of prohibited substances, the Club has a wide-ranging testing programme, which is supported by a world-leading racing laboratory. The laboratory is resourced by leading analytical chemists and equipped with cutting-edge technology and research capabilities;

(4) *Strong Focus on Veterinary Regulation and Equine Care*: the Club ensures the highest level of Veterinary Regulation, with a dedicated Veterinary Regulation, Welfare and Biosecurity Department, together with a

Department of Veterinary Clinical Services, which
delivers ongoing veterinary care to all equine athletes;

(5) *A World-leading Betting Analysis System*: this system,
which uses bespoke computing software, allows
comprehensive and detailed real-time review of betting
information and patterns;

(6) *Disciplinary Structures:* mature, effective and fair
disciplinary measures, procedures and structures.

Finally, it must be noted that the modern sporting landscape
continues to present challenges to the integrity of sport (and
hence, the reputation of sport) which are harder, and more
complex, to address than ever before. One example is the
multi-faceted integrity challenge, posed by the rise in illegal
betting operators and markets, and related criminal networks.
It is estimated that worldwide illegal betting turnover ranges
from US$433 billion to US$3 trillion a year. As with previous
and ongoing threats to the integrity of sport, racing has been a
first-mover to face this issue. Through the Asian Racing
Federation's ground-breaking Anti-Illegal Betting Taskforce,
substantial progress has been made in scoping and understanding the size and nature of the threat posed by illegal betting on
racing and sport through Asia and globally. In the years
ahead, racing will devote significant resources to this challenge, in addition to the many other integrity threats, in order
to maintain its strong reputation and to ensure the ongoing
success of the sport.

OPPORTUNITY OR RISK: A MILLENNIAL'S PERSPECTIVE

Lara Thomas

Consultant, Lansons

Reputation is closely aligned to a business' bottom line. It is also aligned to brand morals and social purpose.

Oxfam's sexual misconduct scandal and VW's emissions scandal, are examples of how public perception is transient, fast and unforgiving. These cases show how profits can be destroyed by hypocritical morals. They also show that pressure from one stakeholder can become a catalyst to wider stakeholder scrutiny and a catalyst to shattering a reputation.

But what if you took millennials, with their widespread use of social media, out of the equation? Would that spark have become smoke? Would we have seen Netflix documentaries, viral YouTube videos and trending hashtags? Or would these issues have remained as boardroom disputes? This shift has been fuelled by a generation with confidence and gravitas pushing for change. Larry Fink of Blackrock reminded us of this in January 2018. Every young generation is engaged in society's ills and plays a role in challenging and fighting these: 1960s — counter culture, the Vietnam war and the use of agent orange; 1980s — Thatcherism and the miner's strikes; and today — social inequality, corporate corruption and individual privacy. The millennial voice is here to stay and it can enforce accountability. For millennials in reputation management this sense of moral duty and integrity underpins their careers.

Reputation management has never been more valuable and the industry has never been more in demand. This industry is about understanding audiences and using the appropriate channels and messaging to shift perceptions. It is about understanding stakeholder's pressure and negotiating their needs and wants. Today all this is arguably more important than ever, as stakeholders have increasing power in making or breaking a reputation.

For the millennial in reputation management, challenging clients and colleagues (with confidence) and holding them to account is commonplace. They have a decisive style. This self-belief comes naturally to millennials − this generation grew up with a continual stream of social media endorsement. Despite this, if an army of millennial reputation managers existed, business would be a hot bed of client-consultant conflict and C-suite-advisor disputes. Businesses have not seen this confidence before. Multi-generational offices have always been important and ever more so for this industry, but now they risk containing parallel workforces. Instead, dynamic duos are important − experienced seniors who can provide the pragmatism and scope that passionate and opinionated millennials sometimes lack. After all, millennials are not budget holders or decision makers, yet.

Back to my first point, with reputation so closely aligned to a business' bottom line, reputation managers must understand business. This will not come from being 'a career PR person' following a vertical ladder through the ranks, but from taking a divergent approach and approaching a career more like a 'jungle gym', in Sheryl Sandberg's words (2013). The switch from journalism or government to PR and communications remains common − increasingly as the media landscape evaporates and tax payer funding tightens — but millennial reputation managers need to be wiser to real business problems. Millennials' lives have experienced a rapid evolution and their careers will be the same. Despite this, media relations will remain a vital skill for what will remain a relationship-driven industry. Not only is media a core channel but the skills associated are transferable and vital. These skills are clear and concise communication, delivered with conviction.

At the risk of dismissing the careers of my older colleagues, it is the legacy of previous generations of PR professionals, which threaten to undermine the strategic value of reputation management. For a millennial these overhangs pose a risk — the perception that a fresh perspective is outweighed by decades of experience; that a career in reputation management can stem only from a career in PR or communications consultancy; that online perceptions represent real life perceptions; and that traditional media is the best channel for successful communication.

No matter where in our career we are, we must always think: what next? For the next generation — what are their drivers? How will they further evolve our industry? Perhaps they will enforce an ethical code of conduct for all reputation managers to abide by? Or perhaps they will have a fluency of the dark web and be there to predict the next wave of challenges?

Our industry is in a permanent state of flux — steered by the public, who drive our client's reputations and the individuals who work to protect and manage these. To succeed, we must anticipate and adapt to this next wave of change.

7

GENDER, DIVERSITY AND REPUTATION MANAGEMENT

As BBC Economics Editor, Kamal Ahmed says, 'organisations perform better if they use all the talent available to them, which means equal opportunity to all people'. This theme underlies this chapter.

I have a lot of sympathy with those who are frustrated that books like this have a diversity chapter. And with Dame Helena Morrissey who writes that she mostly avoids 'women-only' topics.

Unfortunately, we still haven't got there. According to Deloitte, across the world in 2017, only 15% of Board seats were taken up by women. By region, this equates to 22.6% in Europe, 20.8% in Australasia, 18.8% Africa, 14.5% North America, 11.3% Middle East, 7.8% Asia and 7.2% Latin America (2017).

In May 2018, a report for the UK Government found that reasons given by large companies for not appointing women to the Board included 'we've got one already', 'they don't fit in', 'they don't want the hassle' and 'all the good ones have already gone' (Griffiths, 2018). This caused one of my clients to note the irony of Boards insisting on only hiring exceptional women, when for years they've been happy with mediocre men.

I could reel off similar statistics on the lack of inclusivity for people of colour, sexual orientation, physical disability and wealth of background. However, the specific focus for this chapter is to address the subject of reputation management and diversity.

In 'Women and Reputation', Dame Helena Morrissey notes that 'there is still a societal ambivalence towards 'successful' women that can create an obstacle to establishing a positive reputation'.

Best-selling writer, Kate Mosse, who describes her fiction as 'strongly feminist', explains how she works to achieve change through persuasion. She concludes that 'in terms of change, surely it should be the end result that matters, not who gets the credit. I'm more of a quiet revolutionary'.

Kamal Ahmed's latest book, *The Life and Times of a Very British Man* (2018), tells the story of the 1.25 million mixed-race Britons through the prism of Kamal's own life. He discusses how the people at the top of big media organisations don't look like the audience they're trying to serve. This is 'self-defeating, as the big problem in media is reaching a young audience'.

Iain Anderson, Executive Chairman of the Cicero Group writes about his anger when he sees 'rainbow wash'. Examples of brands and businesses who show no ongoing commitment towards LGBT inclusion who simply wrap the rainbow around them, hoping employees and customers will take this at face value.

I believe that the two interviews and two essays in this chapter offer some of the most useful insights in the whole book.

WOMEN AND REPUTATION

Dame Helena Morrissey

Head of Personal Investing, Legal and General Investment Management

I mostly try to avoid 'women-only' topics, awards and panels, preferring to work *with* men towards gender equality rather than segregate us. But I'm convinced that there are specific issues around women's reputations that need acknowledging and addressing as part of our efforts to achieve equality.

Of course, many aspects of reputation are just the same for men and women — it's a vital ingredient of sustained success for anyone, and all of us face an asymmetry between the difficulty and time it takes to build a strong reputation compared with the ease and rapidity with which it can be lost.

But there are also differences. There is still a societal ambivalence towards 'successful' women that can create an obstacle to establishing a positive reputation. There are subtle (and sometimes less subtle) digs, whether in the form of irrelevant media or social media commentary about our appearance, or more serious references around motherhood (or childlessness — it seems we can't win!) The bar for 'good behaviour' can seem higher too. And while I've certainly experienced women being very supportive of each other, we can also be one another's harshest critics, undermining both confidence and reputations. I have been asked painful questions about how I can possibly be a 'good mother' while also pursuing a career — in public, on stage, at moments of vulnerability such as when speaking a long way from home (having only accepted the engagement in the hope of encouraging other women). I am confident that men are not challenged in this way – and don't think I am being oversensitive. Such insinuations are not just personally unsettling but undermine public perceptions and reputations.

But there's little point complaining – let's focus on what we can do to improve things. How can we take more control of our own reputations and become less susceptible to damned-if-she-does, damned-if-she-doesn't criticism? I think we have to accept that there may well be assaults on our reputation – particularly if we are campaigning for change, since that may threaten those who want to maintain the status quo. It's important to avoid rising to the bait on those occasions where we encounter disapproval merely because someone has a different point of view. I've learnt to (mostly) resist the instinctive reaction to respond, especially in anger or in haste, which bestows power on those who are seeking to undermine. And when I've erred in good faith, I remember Theodore Roosevelt's famous speech about the man (or woman!) 'in the arena', 'who errs, who comes short again and again, because there is no effort without error and shortcoming; but who does actually strive to do the deeds'. Not an excuse, but a powerful reminder that if we are genuinely striving for something worthwhile, a stumble should only double our resolve to do better next time – and so restore any damage to our reputation resulting from a genuine mistake.

But it's also important not to enter into a state of denial. We must face justified criticism head on – not shrug off those incidents where we have really messed up. The most underused words in the corporate world are the simple and powerful 'I'm sorry'. A genuine apology goes a long way to rebuilding trust, in turn the pre-requisite to building a lasting reputation. As we take on more influential roles, I'd like to see women setting a new standard, being ready to apologise unequivocally for our mistakes — as well as being less shy about taking the credit for our good deeds. Saying sorry when we know we have erred (and are genuinely committed to learning from the experience) is a sign of strength — and more importantly, of honesty. It's perhaps a sign of how far we have to go that this might seem a bold — and brave — move but it's one that would surely form the basis of a strong and lasting reputation for men and women — and enable us to rise well above those other, petty jibes.

THE QUIET REVOLUTIONARY

Interview with Kate Mosse

Novelist and Playwright

Kate Mosse has sold over eight million books in 38 languages — led by the Languedoc trilogy of Labyrinth, Sepulchre *and* Citadel *— and is a best seller in France, Australia, the USA, Canada, Netherlands, Scandinavia and South Africa as well as her native Britain. Her latest novel,* The Burning Chambers, *was published in May 2018. She is rightly admired for co-founding and leading the Women's Prize for Fiction (initially sponsored by Orange from 1996, then by Baileys from 2014 and now by a partnership of Baileys, Deloitte and NatWest). Her public persona is intelligent, cultured and quintessentially English, like her birthplace of Chichester in Sussex, England. She worked in publishing and as an arts presenter for the BBC, then her 'big break' came when that most mainstream of British institutions — the Richard and Judy television Book Club — 'sprinkled fairy dust' on her and picked her novel,* Labyrinth. *The day after* *the show, it sold 56,000 copies in paperback and went on to be the largest selling book in the UK of 2006.*

Kate identifies as a feminist: 'For me, the "F" word also means "fairness"'. She writes about overlooked women's voices, ordinary women whose stories are often left out of the history books. Her fiction is female led and she wouldn't consider writing a story built *only* around women finding love (hence her preference for Emily Brontë over Austen). She says: 'I want to tell stories about all the things in women's lives'. She also works hard to put 'gentle' men on the page, her theory being that the traditional narrative of active 'heroes' and passive 'heroines' denies both men and women the chance to be themselves. 'I want to reflect the world as it actually is – in its complexity and glory!'

Kate describes her fiction as 'strongly feminist' – in terms of the centrality and independence of her female characters – but wouldn't define it as 'feminist fiction', insofar as the purpose of her writing is to tell stories not to put forward a particular political agenda. This stems from her core belief that 'persuasion, helping people to see another point of view, is more enduring and brings more profound change'. She suggests that while some people's views – on gender, race, faith, policy, social opportunity – are entrenched and unchangeable, others might simply not have engaged with a situation before and therefore are open to persuasion. 'Fiction can often slip between the gaps in a way that nonfiction or political writing cannot'.

When Kate started working in publishing in the mid-1980s, she felt there was still a kind of inverse snobbery in the British literary establishment that tended to believe that high sales were automatically incompatible with quality writing. These days, she suggests that the internet, self-publishing opportunities and the rise of smaller, nimbler independent publishing houses have contributed to a 'democratisation' of literature and criticism. Her own success as a writer in terms of sales means she worries less about her literary reputation in relation to longevity, though Kate admits she always hopes each of her books will hit No 1: 'It is not so much about recognition, but more that the visibility of being in the Top 10 attracts more readers'.

Her 2018 novel, *The Burning Chambers*, is the start of a four-book series that follows the flight of Huguenots from persecution in sixteenth century France to settlements in Franschhoek in nineteenth century South Africa. Though she admits it's hard not to see echoes in the current world situation – destruction of communities, religious and political divisions, dispossession, diaspora – Kate says she doesn't discuss the novel in these terms:

> *Historical fiction must be firmly rooted in the time and place within which it's set. You cannot animate the past with integrity through a 21st century perspective. I'm a storyteller not a polemicist, I want readers to fall in love with the characters and to care about them, not think they're reading a work of history.*

As Deputy Chair of Britain's National Theatre, Kate is well versed in the language of reputation protection and risk registers. After some 30 years of celebrating and promoting other writers' works and reputations, it is not surprising Kate does think consciously about her own reputation, how she presents and particularly how she can utilise her opportunities and position to benefit other writers. Her Twitter profile (which she runs herself – her publishers run her Facebook account) is as an author and supporter of fellow authors.

Kate applauds those who are more outspoken and who campaign proudly and loudly, but her modus operandi is for a quieter, under-the-radar approach and this is reflected in people she admires: director Phyllida Lloyd ('for making things beautiful and accessible'), novelist Toni Morrison ('she refuses to be told what she can or cannot write'), politician Harriet Harman ('responsible for so many firsts and breaking through barriers') and athlete Tanni Grey-Thompson ('for having the courage to be herself and so affect change').

When considering women and society, Kate thinks progress has been slower than expected in some arenas, though is optimistic about the number of young women and men who define themselves as feminists or feminist allies. She welcomes the 'genuine outrage' in Britain over the size of the gender pay gap and the #MeToo movement. She is delighted that the debate about black and minority ethnic representation in the arts is becoming so widespread and hard-hitting and that 'diversity' is being extended to include social background and class. Her steadfast belief remains that a 'plurality of voices' – that's to say making 'room at the table for a wider range of people' – benefits everyone: 'In terms of change, surely it should be the end result that matters, not about who gets the credit. I'm more of a quiet revolutionary'.

A VERY BRITISH MAN

Interview with Kamal Ahmed

BBC Economics Editor

Since 2014, Kamal Ahmed has delivered business and economics news to the British people, firstly as the BBC's Business Editor and currently as its Economics Editor. His path to the role embraced a wide spectrum of newspapers as well as a period in the public sector. He began working as Political Editor of The Observer *newspaper and then as Director of Communications for the Equality and Human Rights Commission. Then, prior to the BBC, he was Business Editor for the Telegraph newspaper group. His first book,* The Life and Times of a Very British Man[13] *was published in October 2018.*

The Life and Times of a Very British Man tells the story of the 1.25 million mixed-race Britons through the prism of Kamal's own life. He is the mixed-race son of an immigrant Sudanese father and an English mother from a traditional background, born in the Northern county of Yorkshire. He was born in 1967 in London, a year before the famous 'Birmingham speech' by right-wing Conservative politician Enoch Powell. The speech foresaw a river 'foaming with blood' if the sons of immigrants, like Kamal, were allowed to remain in the country.

Ahead of the book's publication, I ask Kamal if he's considered the reputational risks to him in taking such a public position on the subjects of race, skin colour and identity. He says, 'I've considered the risks of putting myself in the public domain, in the spotlight, on this subject, and weighed that up against what I hope will be useful'. Adding:

I think I have a privileged position and that comes with a degree of responsibility. Stories of ethnicity are often discussed in binary terms, whereas the mixed-race history of Britain, which my book is in part a celebration of, has been less written about.

The story of mixed-race identity is complex, Kamal says, 'you can simultaneously be proud of our country and yet feel alien in our country'. He adds that 'lots of people have great pride in Britain, whatever their background'. The book plays with the idea that Kamal was living in West London simultaneously loving multi-racial dance group Soul II Soul and traditional British heritage charity, the National Trust. He believes that 'Britishness today is that mix of identities and loves'. He also understands 'the sense of alienation in some "indigenous" people that things have changed too rapidly'. On the book's cover, he is photographed drinking a cup of tea and wearing cufflinks with the logo of legendary 2 Tone Records (the British record label that was home to many multi-racial bands and musical genres). He hopes that the book will 'be received in a nuanced way that adds to the debate we need to have, on identity'.

Talking about his industry, the media, he observes that, 'to this day, the people at the top of big media organisations don't look like the audience they're trying to serve' and that 'things haven't changed sufficiently since the 1990s'. This is self-defeating, as 'the big problem in media is reaching a young audience, we need to listen to them and be aware internally as well as externally of what that means'. Media organisations 'need to find our receive button. Management used to be about broadcasting, ideas, power – now it's about receiving, listening and reacting'.

His days at Britain's Equality and Human Rights Commission convinced him that 'equality matters for everybody'. Organisations perform better if they 'use all the talent available to them, which means equal opportunity to all people'. He adds that:

> *the number of women in senior positions and the debate sparked by #MeToo is progress, but now we need the same on wealth, class and broader diversity including disability, sexuality and age.*

Culture is also hugely important, he says 'if everyone goes to the bar after work, and that's where conversations on business happen, it can exclude whole groups of people, some mothers for example'.

He has great belief in young people, as they 'don't focus on ethnicity and skin colour'. Another difference is that 'younger people won't put up with hurdles being put in their way'. He says, 'when I was young I mostly put up with racist insults because everyone got insulted about something, for me it was skin colour'. However, he believes that young people still face challenges depending on their ethnicity and the views of those living in the capital city, where ethnicity is not, largely, seen as a negative thing, don't always accord with people living in other parts of the country.

In 2008, he wrote of a world 'bursting with astonishing possibilities' after Barack Obama became American President and Lewis Hamilton became Formula One World Champion, because both were, like him, 'black and white' (Ahmed, 2008). He now recognises that it wasn't 'job done'. Adding that we 've learned, 'If we lump people together, generalise too much, we miss the point, people are not on the same journey'. He adds that:

> *you have to listen to the people, the often-quieter group, who may not feel comfortable. If you don't listen, and respond, you can get a reaction that may not have been expecting.*

Reflecting on the impact of Donald Trump, he says that:

> *history is about big waves, slowly developing trends. To many, Obama came at the end of decades of movement in one direction. It's too early to assess whether President Trump is a blip on the chart, or a change in direction.*

'NOT JUST LIP SERVICE – DRIVING CHANGE'

Iain Anderson

Executive Chairman, Cicero Group

The multitude of Pride celebrations all across the globe has become a wonderful moment every year for LGBT people, allies and just ordinary citizens to celebrate a life free from oppression and the right to be just who you are.

My first ever Pride March was in London in the early 1990s and I was conscious I was walking in the footsteps of LGBT activists in the 1960s, 1970s and 1980s who really had helped change the world.

I've marched in Berlin and countless other cities around the world ever since and I never cease to be overwhelmed by watching the sheer joy and acceptance from millions of ordinary people who line the streets of those countless towns and cities to welcome the most visible way of celebrating LGBT freedoms.

Increasingly business has wanted to get involved to show commitment towards a diverse and accepting workplace by sponsoring floats and encouraging LGBT workplace groups.

Last year I found myself on London's Pride march with the global CEO of a FTSE company. An LGBT ally himself, he was the only FTSE CEO on the march. But I could not help but pinch myself. Just a few years ago that would have seemed impossible.

Countless others business leaders marched but another of the most uplifting sights is to see soldiers, police, fire crews and other public servants decked out with a rainbow logo leading from the front.

I have no time for those who say this is just gesturing. I think of when I joined the workplace – over 20 years after male homosexuality was legalised in the UK – and I did not feel I could be 'out'. Employers didn't provide any signalling or support then.

Today, employers are making a tangible commitment to demonstrate they want to encourage people to be just who they are at work, which is a huge step forward. Last year, I was invited to speak to one of the UK's main employer bodies, the Institute of Directors, to help launch their Pride in Business network. A huge rainbow flag was extended outside their headquarters in the most 'old establishment' part of London. Some change has taken place in my lifetime.

Of course I am conscious that some of the desire to 'wrap the rainbow' around business is part of 'brand' management. Especially around 'employer brand' management in terms of recruitment and talent. It is also about the changing nature of customers too. Again, three cheers from me.

In particular, millennial customers are asking a lot more from the businesses they work for and the brands they buy from. A commitment towards LGBT inclusion has become an important part of that.

But where I do get angry is when I see 'rainbow wash'. Examples of brands and businesses who show no ongoing commitment towards LGBT inclusion who simply wrap the rainbow around them hoping employees and customers will take this at face value.

In fact – given my personal visibility on these issues and as a corporate adviser – many companies often ask me if they should get involved with Pride or other high-profile

LGBT events. Many of those calls I receive at the last minute in a desperate rush to 'join the herd'. My advice is simple: are you able to show your active commitment across your workforce and across your entire business towards inclusion? If you can't – start to do so and get involved in the future.

It's only been a few years since I decided to make inclusion a part of my own employer brand but I am very proud of the recognition we have received from awards, our employees and from the businesses we work with. Since doing so, our business is significantly larger and I wish we had done it years ago.

But there is much more to do. I have recently become part of a new effort – GiveOUT[14] – a charity supporting LGBT activities in countries where currently rights don't exist or are actually going backwards.

Anyone running a business in Russia at the moment or in 37 of the 53 Commonwealth countries knows that fostering LGBT inclusion at work is almost impossible. More than the tenor of much of global politics right now shows there are two camps developing: countries where diversity and tolerance are accepted and countries where they are in reverse.

The power of reputation and the power of global investors is key here. Watching many global companies push back against countries pushing repressive policies is vital here and I am delighted to see so many firms doing just that. Investor action will move policy faster than anything else.

Whether its brand, reputation, investor or customer power that moves the dial – we have now reached a new and crucial stage in the journey of 'rainbow power'.

8

THE REPUTATION MANAGEMENT TOOLKIT

All organisations are currently managing their reputation. Very few are managing them in a holistic, integrated way.

There are several available frameworks for those considering a more integrated approach for the first time. John Doorley has copyrighted his aptly named 'Comprehensive Reputation Management' framework and that's a good place to start (2011).

At the end of this chapter, Kaspar Ulf Nielsen, Chief Product Officer of the Reputation Institute outlines his approach to 'Building the Reputational Competencies Needed to Succeed'. He includes fascinating case studies of how Allstate Insurance and Novo Nordisk have used the framework to reputational advantage.

The reputation management toolkit I have developed for this book has five key elements:

(1) Organisational structure

(2) Measurement and insight

(3) Goals and accountability

(4) The plan

(5) The programmes:
  - 'Doing the right thing'.

  - 'Telling the best story'.

  - 'Delighting customers, retailers and intermediaries'.

  - 'Influencing the influencers'.

  - 'Risk mitigation and crisis preparedness'.

The diagram below shows the complete reputation management toolkit, and just how many complex elements are involved in delivering the best reputation an organisation can have (**Diagram 4**).

For the rest of the chapter, we'll concentrate on some of the key issues involved in delivering an effective programme (see **Diagram 4** on the next page).

REMUNERATION POLICY

Remuneration policies, including bonuses and other incentivisations, are crucial in determining how an organisation behaves. If these are not aligned to 'doing the right thing', then, unfortunately, it won't happen. As Charlie Munger, Warren Buffet's long-term business partner said, 'show me the incentive and I'll show you the outcome' (Pape and Whittaker, 2018).

If an organisation is dedicated to delighting customers, then customer satisfaction has to form an element of the CEO's bonus. If call centre staff are measured by how short their average call length is, then customers won't be delighted.

Call centres that are constantly busy haven't employed enough staff, in the interest of profit and efficiency, so the

Diagram 4. Repuation Management Toolkit.

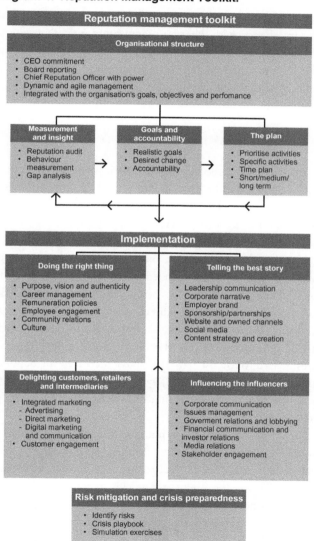

© Tony Langham 2018

organisations shouldn't have 'putting customers at the centre of our world' as a core value.

Unless the remuneration, incentivisation and bonus policies are aligned with what an organisation says it's trying to do, then that organisation can never be authentic. So, an effective reputation management programme should influence remuneration policy.

DYNAMIC, FLEXIBLE AND AGILE

Many older professionals remind their younger colleagues that managing reputation is in some ways the same now as it has always been. The most authentic organisations always performed better than others. Communication has always been about telling great stories.

There's some truth in this. But in many more ways, reputation management has changed beyond almost all recognition and continues to change. Social media has increased the pace. Customers having direct and public access has increased the intensity of praise and anger. Modern NGOs and organisations such as the International Consortium of Investigative Journalist[15] (ICIJ) – have increased the depth of challenge. AI will exponentially multiply the scale of criticism. All this in an increasingly dissatisfied and unsympathetic world.

For these reasons, the reputation management structure should be agile, dynamic and flexible. This should be self-evident, but in late 2017, according to McKinsey, 'organizational agility – the ability to quickly reconfigure strategy, structure, processes, people, and technology – is proving elusive for most'. Their research showed that only 4% of organisations had completed an agile transformation although 37% had one underway. They concluded that organisational agility is 'catching fire'. For those wanting to deliver effective reputation management, organisational transformation is essential.

WE CAN'T BORE OUR STAKEHOLDERS (OR EACH OTHER)

One of the dangers in professionalising (and even creating) a function like reputation management is that a new bureaucracy is created in addition to the existing siloes. And there are already too many of those.

As discussed in Chapter 5, companies require two things from the range of professions we call 'marketing services': profitable revenue and a strong reputation. There need only be two core functions: integrated marketing and reputation management. In addition to an insight function with the skills and weight to measure reputation, as well as the data analytics required for marketing. This should reduce bureaucracy, not create more.

In reputation management, as in everything else, the work, in terms of time taken, should be 5% strategy and 95% implementation.

And our new structures need to leave greater scope for creativity to flourish. The new head of reputation management should be just as much fun over a coffee as the old head of public relations.

This latter point while flippant, contains a heartfelt belief. There is a danger that reputation management comes to symbolise 'reputation protection' only. It shouldn't.

RISK MITIGATION AND CRISIS PREPAREDNESS

Crises are now an inevitability for almost every organisation over a 10-year period and are therefore inevitable parts of every CEO and CCO's career. Risk mitigation and crisis preparedness now form part of every organisation's ongoing activity. For this reason, crisis management is discussed separately in Chapter 10.

ETHICS AND COMMUNICATION

Ethics, and the overlapping but also separate areas of legality and morality, are becoming critical areas for everyone in business life, particularly those of us working in reputation management.

I completely reject the idea that what we do might be unethical in itself. In a modern capitalist economy, democracy is strengthened if all elements of society openly communicate. Democracy is weakened by secrecy and opacity. If companies communicate, that is good for society. If they lobby Government, that is how democracy works. But society should be able to see who lobbies who, and how much they spend.

In the international arena, the same holds true. Countries that communicate and explain are preferable to those that don't.

The ethics (or more correctly morality) of who we work for, as individuals or consultancies, is a matter of individual conscience. Tobacco companies, casinos, high interest lenders, fracking companies and mining companies are OK to some, unacceptable to others. As long as the activity is legal, it seems to me a matter of personal choice who someone works for or represents. In consultancies, however, I believe that there should be an individual conscience option. Just because the consultancy decides to work for a fracking company, it doesn't follow that all members of staff have to work on that piece of business. They should be allowed the option to decline.

There are three areas of ethics that I feel strongly about. They are: transparency, what we actually do and 'fake news'.

Reputation managers should be transparent about who they are working for, at all times, when the work is in the public domain. Principally this means when engaging with journalists, lobbying Government or trying to influence debates of public interest. For those people working for companies, Government or other organisations this is relatively straightforward. Although it does mean that the formation of 'fake' interest groups or (not actually) 'independent' expert websites is automatically wrong.

For those working in consultancies, this means declaring our clients when we work in the public domain. It's simply not acceptable to conceal them.

When UK-based consultancy Bell Pottinger imploded in 2017, it wasn't because it had worked for Oakbay Investments, the South African company owned by the Gupta Brothers. It imploded because the 'economic emancipation' campaign it worked on, was seen to incite racial hatred. What we, as reputation management professionals, actually do for our clients is key. And we need to do the right thing just as we often advise our clients to.

For many consumer brands, it's very tempting to concoct stories that fit the 'clickbait' obsession of some media outlets. It can seem harmless. At the opposite extreme, the deliberate release of knowingly fake news to influence election results is clearly wrong. As a profession, we should be part of neither.

ONLINE REPUTATION MANAGEMENT, MEDIA RELATIONS AND THE USE OF LAWYERS

There are three areas of reputation management that I wanted to probe in more detail and the three excellent essays that follow do just that.

Founder of Digitalis, Dave King argues that today 'there is a strong argument that your *online* reputation *is* your reputation'. The danger is that 'unintentionally, Google has become a filtration system which allows the negative content to rise to the top and stick'

Top London journalist Simon English discusses how CEOs handle the media. He argues that the CEOs with the best reputation among journalists are the ones who are 'most open, most human, most able to admit that they don't know everything'.

Working alongside a client's lawyers has become an increasing part of my reputation management work. So I'm delighted that Mishcon Partner Emma Woollcott shares the lawyer's perspective for this book.

The chapter is completed by Kasper Ulf Nielsen, Chief Product Officer of the Reputation Institute who outlines his approach to Building the Reputational Competencies Needed to Succeed. He includes fascinating case studies of how Allstate Insurance and Novo Nordisk have used the framework to build reputational advantage.

ONLINE REPUTATION MANAGEMENT

Dave King

Founder, Digitalis

Interest from all stakeholders in an individual or organisation comes in one of two forms: cursory research or due diligence. If the target person is well-known, there may be preconceived beliefs or opinions on the part of the researcher; those unknowns begin with no such preconception but with the blank canvas of enquiry. Irrespective, those enquiries inevitably begin online. Google (and its limited competition) is inevitably now the primary influencer of the opinions formed by journalists, investors and customers. The vast majority of those who dig deeper (investigators and due diligence providers) rely increasingly on online sources, sometimes still coupled with human source enquiries. Even the primary sources of information on individuals, which are *not* openly available online – the subscription-based databases provided for example by those who provide KYC (Know Your Customer) compliance services to financial institutions – in turn source the majority of their own information from the open web. As such, there is a strong argument that today, your *online* reputation *is* your reputation.

Cursory research tends to be limited to the tip of the iceberg that is the front page of Google, whereas more sophisticated scrutiny could reach the deepest corners of the deep, unindexed and even dark web. Those 10 or 20 articles or

web pages contained in the top pages of a search are determined entirely by the whims of a third-party algorithm, while
the vast underbelly of content elsewhere on the web can be
supplemented by anyone, anywhere, at any time. As a result,
two primary service lines have spawned in the nascent area of
online reputation management: (1) SERP (Search Engine
Results Page) management and (2) the monitoring and management of what might be found in the deeper web. Both are
increasingly automated in their delivery and the early tricks
and tools used by an increasing number of prominent people
and businesses are instructive in terms of predicting the future
of (online) reputation management.

Google aims to rank the most relevant or interesting content for any given search phrase, using as its frame of reference, among other metrics, the extent to which people have
linked to or liked one article or page, relative to another.
Sadly, human nature means the sensationalist and negative
content is more interesting than its benign counterparts so,
albeit unintentionally, Google has become a filtration system
which allows the negative content to rise to the top and stick.
Unmanaged, then, all our profiles look worse rather than
better. Those who manage their profiles proactively will
already create strong, well-optimised content around their
commercial, social and philanthropic endeavours, actively
promoting the same in key search engines and often using
technology to displace any erroneous or negative content.
That technology will track the same metrics as are used by
search engine algorithms, determining how the natural trajec-
tory of salacious criticism might best be offset.

Technology, too, plays an increasing role in managing —
or at least mitigating the impact of — the content buried
away in the deep web. There are already many platforms
which allow the routine monitoring of a name or subject.
Those which are more sophisticated provide some level of

alert system for rapid notification of a new issue which might be flagged somewhere on the internet. Today, human analysis and response is often needed and many types of content are difficult to remedy – though in such cases awareness at least facilitates preparedness.

These technologies, as ever in a nascent market, have barely scratched the surface of their own potential and their continued development will be at the heart of the future of online reputation management – and therefore of reputation management as a whole. Managing one's profile on search engines will increasingly use AI, as will the rapid identification of – and to an extent the management of – the many threats which originate in some far-flung corner of the web. This is an area already seeing huge development, partly driven by the command of one's reputation held by specific third parties. But add in the increasing frequency – and sophistication – of targeted reputational attacks on individuals and organisations and somewhat of an arms race ensues.

CEOs AND THE MEDIA: 'TELL THE TRUTH, IT'S EASIER TO REMEMBER'

Simon English
Senior City Correspondent, Evening Standard

In *The West Wing*, the estimable drama about how much better the world could be if our leaders were the best of us – the smartest, most decent and most far sighted folk available – the President and his staff worry about his legacy.

Even though this administration are plainly the best people to be in charge — a (highly) idealised imagination of the Clinton Presidency — they fret about reputation management.

At some point, they realise this isn't getting them anywhere. The obsession with polls and market testing just holds back the President from being himself. President Bartlet is not without flaws — he's human — but he refrains from saying what he thinks, because pollsters tell him it won't play well.

Since he isn't playing well anyway, a decision is reached. To hell with it.

Chief of staff, Leo McGarry calls the senior staff together.

He tells them: 'We're not going to be threatened by issues: we're going to put 'em front and centre. We're gonna raise the level of public debate in this country, and let *that* be our legacy. That sound alright to you?'

The President decides that rather than worrying about his reputation, he's just going to do the right thing.

Perhaps not much reputation management is needed if you're decent in the first place. If issues engulf you and you lose anyway, well, that's just tough. If you can't cope with that possibility, don't apply to be chief executive.

I think of this sometimes when in the midst one of those tedious interviews with chief executives that I endure all the time. This guy has nothing to say. Or if he does, he isn't going to say them. Why did he phone me to repeat what is on the statement I have already read?

In the background lurk PR folk who are mostly concerned with avoiding disaster. They are the equivalent of a football manager who thinks a nil-nil draw is a great result.

CEOs don't have to be particularly charismatic. But they must surely be able to talk more freely about the businesses they run than they do.

The CEOs with the best reputation among journalists are the ones who are most open, most human and most able to admit that they don't know everything that sometimes they get things wrong.

The ones with the worst reputation ramble, dissemble, worry way too much about the press, have no sense of humour and hide behind jargon.

The chief executive who doesn't care too much what I'm going to write is a wise man. Later on, he'll be right and I'll be wrong. Unless he really is useless, in which case no amount of reputation management is going to save him.

In my opinion, women bosses seem naturally better at this stuff. In the UK, Jayne-Anne Gadhia at Virgin Money, Liv Garfield at Severn Trent and Alison Cooper at Imperial Brands, all seem to come across as human without much effort.

As if they were just trying to do a good job. Perhaps they are.

For this, they should get the benefit of the doubt when things aren't going their way. Perhaps as much as another year in the job before the critics really get their teeth in. Sadly, women chief executives have a harder time. They can't just represent themselves, but a whole gender. Things are changing, thankfully.

When the opportunity arose to bash Top Shop boss Sir Philip Green and WPP's Sir Martin Sorrell, they got precisely two minutes of grace before the press piled in.

Why? Because their reputations as bullies preceded them. They thought the way to good press was to menace. It worked. For quite a long while.

The reputations of both of them are now tarnished beyond what they think is fair and are unlikely to fully recover. They have only themselves to blame.

Have I ever been falsely charmed by a CEO or a politician who later turned out to be up to no good? Guilty, as charged. But the truth always came out in the end.

Even when he was regarded as the banker of the age, before everything collapsed, being dragged across town to be

y then Royal Bank of Scotland boss Fred Goodwin
.ut as much fun as an endoscopy.

.ere's something wrong with this bloke, thought everyone, apart from, apparently, the people charged with protecting his reputation.

Goodwin treated the press with disdain. Not good-
natured scepticism, disdain. When he needed friends, he
found he had none.

None of this should be mysterious. From the outside,
reputation management can look like industries doing nothing more sophisticated than making platitudes out of the
obvious. That or putting lipstick on a pig.

So, how's this as a one-line plan for good PR: Tell the
truth. If nothing else, it is the easiest thing to remember.

REPUTATION MANAGEMENT: THE LAWYER'S PERSPECTIVE

Emma Woollcott

Partner, Mishcon de Reya

Most high-profile media stories involve the disclosure of
information which the subject would wish remained confidential, or allegations they consider impugn their good name.
Both potentially breach the subject's rights — but may be justified in the public interest and to uphold the freedom of
expression. And therein starts the endless balancing exercise
between competing legal rights.

Over time, the courts as well as the pendulum of public
opinion seem to swing between championing privacy and
respect for confidentiality, and then heralding as sacrosanct

freedom of speech and the freedom of the press. The past few years have seen:

- the rise and fade (and potential resurgence) of the 'super-injunction' (where the court prohibits publication of private or confidential information, as well as the fact of an injunction having been obtained);

- a raising of the bar in relation to the 'serious harm' required to initiate defamation proceedings in the courts of England and Wales; and

- an intended tightening of the requirements to bring a publication within the jurisdiction of the English courts, to avoid claims of 'libel tourism'.

Tougher press regulation was promised following the phone-hacking scandal and Part 1 of the UK's Leveson Inquiry[16] but, with competing systems of self-regulation and the government's decision to scrap Leveson Part 2, the transitory caution prompted by a spotlight being cast on press behaviour and journalistic standards appears to have ebbed. There is an increasing sense among practitioners that even mainstream media organisations are abandoning established standards of good journalistic practice, potentially in an attempt to compete with online platforms and independent publishers.

In a world of fake news, social media trolling and fast-moving, global stories, the law is sometimes criticised for failing to keep up with modern technology, or for being ineffective in its application to modern reputational crises. However, this view fails to take account of the scope and breadth of the legal tools available to those who are well-prepared and bold enough to use them. Whether the complaint is grounded in defamation, privacy, harassment, data protection, conspiracy or any other legal basis, intelligent and decisive action is crucial. Judges are increasingly alive to the challenges of internet publications across multiple jurisdictions, including the particular dynamics of social media.

When in the spotlight, it is easy to lose sight of the bigger picture and to focus only on those currently on the attack. With politically driven agendas and vendettas being pursued aggressively through multiple channels, and a public clamouring for punishment and disgrace, those who face reputational challenges and scrutiny need to pick their battles wisely, and remain focused on the long and medium term, as well as the urgent. Carefully considered, measured and strategic legal (and coordinated PR) engagement with key stakeholders, regulators (which are increasingly being weaponised), publishers and social media platforms can help to contain or shape a story, and minimise lasting reputational damage.

With traditional publishers being concerned to mitigate the financial consequences of getting it wrong, it is arguably easier to secure corrections, updates and apologies – and to influence how a story is followed up.

Although sceptics predicted the digital age would see the end of the media injunction (the theory being that material spreads faster online than it can be contained) recent experience suggests that this powerful remedy remains available and effective. Last year, we secured what was reported to be the first ever 'fake news' injunction against a 'person unknown', namely the author of an anonymous and concerted email and social media campaign to circulate doctored media stories. The injunction (to prevent harassment and defamation) was served by email and effective immediately, thwarting what appeared to be escalating into a potentially ruinous attack. As the Supreme Court has recently confirmed, the right to privacy relates not only to the keeping of secrets but to the protection against intensive media scrutiny and intrusion. Privacy law, therefore, has a role to play even where the cat is already partly out of the bag.

Tracing those who would seek to avoid detection online is challenging — but often possible through a combination of forensic technical and legal applications. The courts can order disclosure from those innocently embroiled in the wrong-doing of others — including against ISPs, domain hosts and mobile phone providers who hold IP and other data which may be used to identify anonymous publishers.

Whatever the reputational crisis, the ability to respond quickly but intelligently is critical. Readiness and courage are key. Those who fare best in the eye of the storm are those who are prepared, and who are brave enough, to steer their own ship.

BUILDING THE REPUTATION COMPETENCIES NEEDED TO SUCCEED

Kasper Ulf Nielsen
Chief Product Officer, Reputation Institute

The world has become more complex, fragmented and fast-paced. We have 24/7 news, nonstop social media buzz and stakeholder activism in every corner of the world. This chaos of information makes it extremely challenging to get the clarity needed to make the right decisions.

Who should you pay attention to?

Where are your risks?

Where should you invest time, focus and money?

This complexity makes reputation management even more difficult. So, what should you do?

The answer is not more data. The answer is developing the structures and competencies inside the organisation to gather the right reputation intelligence, and have the skills needed to develop action from the data.

The success of any organisation over the next years will be to build out robust reputation management capabilities inside the organisation. It is not enough to design a reputation management system. Companies need to invest in the competencies needed to engage and communicate with stakeholders in a way that displays how the company delivers on its core purpose and provides shared value to all audiences.

THE FOUR ELEMENTS OF REPUTATION EXCELLENCE FRAMEWORK

For companies to achieve their business goals, they need support from stakeholders. They need customers to buy and recommend their products. They need the financial community to invest in their company. They need the regulators to provide them the licence to operate and they need employees to deliver on the strategy. If they do this, the company will have success. In return, these stakeholders want to be able to trust the company to deliver on their promises. And that is at the heart of reputation.

So, the big question is how to develop a trusted relationship with key stakeholders? How do you take the right actions towards the different groups and how do you ensure you get your great stories told in a way that builds the awareness and knowledge about who you are as a company and not just what you sell and produce?

Diagram 5. The Reputation Journey.

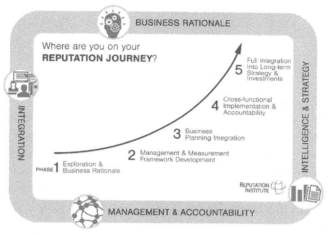

Source: Reputation Institute.

From studying the global members of our Reputation Leaders Network, we have identified four key competencies needed to manage the corporate reputation and gain competitive advantage (**Diagram 5**).

BUSINESS RATIONALE

The first element has to do with the business case. Who are the key stakeholders you need support from to achieve your business goals? What specific action do you want these people to take for you? What is the financial benefit/risk from these actions? And how does this align with the overall value and strategy of the company?

Managing your reputation is about upside and downside. And the leaders know what financial impact their reputation has with their most important stakeholders.

INTELLIGENCE AND STRATEGY

The second element is focused on insights and strategy. Now that you know who the most critical stakeholders are, and what the financial impact of their perception is, then you need to define what they want from you and how they see you today. What is your reputation with each stakeholder? Where do you have major risks? Where are your opportunities? And what do you need to say and do to win their trust and support?

For this to make sense, you need to have one common framework from which to analyse perception. Each stakeholder is different but you need to be able to develop a consistent framework and align strategy across stakeholders to build a strong and targeted strategy for reputation.

MANAGEMENT AND ACCOUNTABILITY

The third element is focused on activating reputation management across the organisation. It is not possible to manage your reputation from one central department. Building trust with clients, partners, regulators, investors and employees happens on a day-to-day basis across the entire organisation. Successful reputation management is where people across the organisation take ownership of building trust with their own stakeholders. They have access to the intelligence from the reputation research, they know what the drivers of reputation are, and they use the proof points in their communication and actions towards the different stakeholders.

With this in place, the leading companies have local KPIs for reputation moving the ownership and accountability into the marketplace and not just in the corporate realm.

INTEGRATION

The fourth element has to do with integrating all of this knowledge into action and communication across all the right touch points and channels. Stakeholders form their opinion based on their own direct experiences with the company, what they hear from the company and what they hear other people say about the company. Successful reputation management requires an integrated approach across all of these touch points. It is not enough to do good corporate communication or public relations. The leading companies integrate their reputation strategy and narrative across all touch points, from the day-to-day conversation with a client, to large scale corporate branding campaigns.

MOVING FORWARD ON YOUR REPUTATION JOURNEY

Reputation management is a journey. Every organisation is different and the reputation journey is not a linear or sequential exercise. Depending on where you and your company are on this journey, you can and should take different next steps (**Diagram 6**).

If you are just starting on your journey, then you need to develop a business case for moving forward. Who are the key stakeholders you need support from, what is the expected

Diagram 6. Reputation Competency Framework.

Source: Reputation Institute.

financial impact from this, and where do you stand today? Without this data driven platform you will have difficulty getting the support from the executive group to invest behind reputation management.

If you have been measuring reputation for some time, but want to leverage the insights to inform actions and communications then you need to apply a more in-depth analytical approach to how you link data, communication and outcome. You should link the messages you send with the outcome from stakeholders to get the highest return on investment from your research, marketing and communication budgets.

And if you are at a stage where you are ready to start putting reputation on the bonus plan of your CEO and report on reputation in the annual report, then you need to develop a systematic plan for how your reputation data can be audited by the external accountant, and be presented in a dashboard to the executive committee and the Board of Directors.

Becoming a Phase 4 or 5 company is not a destination or an outcome. It's a skillset which enables the organisation to make faster decisions, deal with risk in greater confidence, create alignment between activities, report on reputation and increase the return on investments.

Mastering the reputation competency framework enables business leaders to act with the clarity and confidence needed to make the right decision every time.

Case: Novo Nordisk

When it comes to understanding the financial impact of reputation, few companies can equal Danish pharmaceutical company Novo Nordisk. The executive team as well as staff colleagues at all levels understand the value of a strong reputation across key stakeholders and this fuels the work to continuously develop the competencies for how to build trust and support across the company. It was this focus on long-term value creation that set in motion the development of the Novo Nordisk Reputation Intelligence and Management programme.

The executive group together with the Board of Directors wanted to ensure that the company was actively integrating a multi-stakeholder perspective across the company. To ensure this, the Corporate Communication team developed the blueprint for how the company should manage its reputation with key stakeholders around the world.

Novo Nordisk took point of departure in the Reputation Competency Framework to identify where the company stood and what needed to be improved. Through a systematic assessment of the business case for each stakeholder, a mapping of existing perception research conducted across the company, a definition of key performance indicators and collaboration with key function leaders, the company created a cross-functional reputation dashboard that guides actions.

With the framework, Novo Nordisk now have a systematic way of listening to people across the business, and with this comes the clarity to improve communication and engagement with key stakeholders across the company. But even more importantly, Novo Nordisk has a common understanding for how our corporate brand and reputation drives business success at the local level. It's not seen as just a corporate programme but also as a valuable tool for local business development, and that is where I think we will see strong results from our new approach.

With the Novo Nordisk Reputation Intelligence and Management blueprint the company now have a clear and consistent way of monitoring the trust and support across stakeholders and countries. And from this, the company now have alignment inside the different functions on what each can do to secure the support needed to reach the overall business goals of the company.

Case: Allstate Insurance Company

Corporate reputation has always been important at Allstate Insurance Company, America's largest publicly traded property and casualty insurance company. It wasn't until the late 2000s though — in the aftermath of Hurricane Katrina — that the company truly dedicated itself to corporate reputation as a management discipline.

With a mandate from senior leadership, Allstate began its new reputation journey by proving the business case for reputation. That business case, combined with a cross-stakeholder measurement framework, created the foundation of Allstate's reputation strategy which leverages stakeholder data to drive targeted engagement and business results.

This approach has enabled powerful reputation-building initiatives to emerge, ranging from launching an employee Ambassador programme with more than 6,000 participants, to supporting the development of Good Hands Roadside Assistance and Allstate's Claims Satisfaction Guarantee, as well as rolling-out highly tailored local community programmes.

Allstate wants to inspire and enable more leaders to proactively use stakeholder and reputation insights to build more effective strategies and business plans. Leaders need to be aware of how collective decision-making can build or harm the reputation and business. To support the decision-making process Allstate is using the reputation insights to drive decision-making and have three criteria to assess the impact of an initiative:

(1) They hit at least two or three of our key reputation drivers with customers and are also meaningful to other stakeholders;

(2) They target areas where the majority of our target audiences are open to changing their perceptions of us; and

(3) They highlight ideas in which Allstate has existing credibility and advocates.

With this approach, Allstate is ensuring the insights from the reputation research drive better action, which in turn will increase trust and support from customers and other key stakeholders.

9

CASE STUDIES FROM THE BEST OF THE BEST

When researching this book among students, the number one request was for case studies. But not just those that appear in most reputation and crisis management books, like Johnson & Johnson (J&J), BP, VW, Samsung, etc.

To cater for this, we approached the world's leading reputation managers. We asked them to describe, in around 250 words, the time they made the most difference to an organisation or individual reputation.

I'm absolutely thrilled to be able to showcase 39 of those case studies here. Specially written for this book, we have six case studies from the Americas, 21 from Europe, five from Africa and the Middle East and seven from the Asia/Pacific region. In total, we have case studies from practitioners based in 28 different countries.

As a reputation management professional, the most joyous thing is to be reminded of the great work our industry is involved in, all around the world.

Dirk Aarts

Managing Partner at 24/7 Communication, Poland, Europe

Case: Me. I Work at McDonald's!

In Poland, 10 years ago, this sentence wouldn't have been spoken with the exclamation mark, or with lots of self-confidence. Yet today, people working at McDonald's restaurants are proud to say so.

Flash back to 2006: Even having an outstanding reputation of product quality, operations and management, McDonald's was not considered seriously as a place of work by many people who were looking for a job. Perceptions of demanding work, moderate conditions, irregular working times and limited career options were causing an unfavourable reputation of the work place. Operating in the service sector where people play a key role, McDonald's decided to make serious work of their employer brand, and trusted my agency to support them.

A clear-cut Employer Value Proposition was defined. Key messages were set out. Target segmentation was introduced, differentiating strategies towards diverse groups of employees. A wide series of creative initiatives were implemented, varying from design of a uniform by fashion designers to open days, and internal competitions. Engagement, transparency, straightforwardness and consistency were key drivers of change.

But the most successful and absolute game-changer throughout the years was our – at that time – pioneering strategy to have real employees featured in the campaigns. Employees who no longer were hiding, but proudly being the face of McDonald's work place. They told *their* story. Showed *their* passion, *their* drive. They? They work at McDonald's! Still today they are driving McDonald's reputation as one of Poland's most attractive employers in its segment.

Rania Azab

Founder and CEO of 4PR Group, Egypt

Case: Go Bus

A tragic accident resulting in 6 dead and 20 injured, created an emotional crisis with families and media blaming Go Bus for the death of their loved ones. Videos of speeding buses, drivers on cell phones, boycott pages, calls to revoke their licence, affected not only online sales but also left the brand at its lowest credibility levels with high online negativity at 80%.

4PR Group was assigned to restore Go Bus' reputation by rebuilding trust and making the brand likeable again.

A campaign was developed engaging media and the public with Go Bus in a series of events to showcase the state of the art operations and to experience the brand, transforming them into Go Bus influencers by posting their experience on social media and inviting others to join. The campaign started with two media visits to show muscles: the drivers' training in certified Egyptian training centre and a presentation at the control unit during the fleet trip to the 'World Youth forum'.

Followed by public activations in high profile events, Go Bus offered special trips to the African Championship and World Cup qualification matches as well as being the official sponsor and carrier of the Luxor charity Marathon to build a cancer hospital.

Trips were supported by live feeds of Go Bus fleets, passengers' celebrating the experience, celebrity testimonials, organic hype and conversation and strong media coverage.

This resulted in an immediate sentiment flip and high engagement of 80% and 22,293,500 impressions.

The Go Bus campaign restored its image with its online business increasing to 90%.

Madan Badal

Managing Director, AdFactors PR, India

Case: The Konkan Railway

The context: In 1993, Indian railway's plan to build a self-funded railway line on the west coast ran into a negative media campaign around its viability and environmental impact. The executive agency, the Konkan Railway Corporation Limited (KRCL) was to raise money through a public offer of tax-free bonds. Individual investors did not understand tax-free bonds, a first of its kind instrument.

The strategy: Our strategy consisted of three elements: positioning, influencer outreach and innovation across the communications process.

The execution:

- Our positioning underscored the national importance of the project. We made individual presentations to more than 100 luminaries, including national sportsmen, business leaders, environmentalists, politicians and academics. Their voices in support were published in advertisements in leading dailies.

- We briefed the editors of India's leading newspapers, where we contested the negative campaign and expounded the merits.

- We canvassed support with 60,000 investors in Mumbai whose family name suggested roots in the catchment areas.

- Lastly, in an audacious influencer outreach programme, we individually briefed 16,500 chartered accountants, 300 banking leaders and 400 cash-rich businesses, detailing the superior yield of the tax-free bond compared to other debt products.

- This was supported with six advertising campaigns customised for different audiences.

- We creatively leveraged the railway infrastructure to promote the offer.

The results: The KRCL offer was over-subscribed; KRCL was able to raise money later at fine rates. *The Economic Times*, India's largest business newspaper, hailed the communications campaign by Adfactors in an eight-column front page story.

Beth Balsam

Founder and CEO, X2PR, USA

Case: Duracell – Toys for Tots

Like many businesses that rely on holiday gifting, fourth quarter sales have a huge impact on Duracell's business as parents buy battery operated toys for their children. We were challenged with elevating the Duracell name during this critical quarter and by doing so, giving parents a reason to pick our brand over the competition.

Duracell had a long-standing partnership with Toys for Tots, but so did many other brands. We needed to elevate above the noise and give Duracell its own share of voice.

To do this we negotiated a deal with Ellen DeGeneres and had her launch the campaign in November 2013 in a highly branded and visual way. We chose Van Nuys airport in Los Angeles as our event location. The star of the show – other than Ellen – was a C-130 cargo plane that we wrapped to resemble a Duracell Copper Top battery. At the event, Ellen and some local children handed off cases of Duracell batteries to the Marines to symbolically kick of the Toys for Tots programme.

This was followed by four integrations on her popular show between Thanksgiving and Christmas. Each of those show integrations included a retail partner, which helped Duracell secure favourable displays and shelf space at their top customer stories.

This campaign not only helped Duracell own share of voice with more than one billion media impressions, but also successfully helped the brand to own the quarter from a retail visibility and sales perspective.

Michaela Benedigova, PhD

Managing Director and Partner, SeeSame, Slovakia

Case: First Aid for Reputation

Hardly anyone likes the pharmaceutical industry. Most people have a negative view of the pharmaceutical industry believing pharmaceutical companies are only interested in profit. Pfizer in Slovakia was looking for an effective antidote to the unfavourable reputation with their key stakeholders, institutions and public. The idea of the campaign was born out of our personal experience. We have all been in situations when our own life or the lives of our relatives were in danger. Based on rescue workers' estimate, only 5% of Slovaks give first aid before the ambulance arrives.

We decided to make a difference and teach as many people as possible to save lives using their bare hands. And so, a Land of Saviours was born — a place where everybody is capable of providing first aid effectively and without hesitation.

We joined forces and developed new communication channels and a brand-new system of theoretical and practical first aid training online, creating the most freely available educational platform. Pfizer has been on a long journey leading to a genuine change in the attitude of the lives and wellbeing of others and their loved ones with no expectation of profit or sales increase. The campaign helped Pfizer significantly improve its reputation, dialogue with direct project partners as well as its supporters (The Parliamentary Healthcare Committee, health professionals, patients' organisations, insurance companies, media and employers).

The Land of Saviours united organisations and individuals under one universally beneficial objective: saving lives.

Rosanna D'Antona

President, Havas PR Milan, Italy

Case: Ferrarelle

Ferrarelle is a historical Italian natural sparkling mineral water producer, who focus their attention on source protection and the environment. They are well-established, reliable and involved in positive causes through culture, art, health and research. Its stakeholders, including the financial community know the company and its leaders well. This reputation has allowed Ferrarelle to be considered as a trustful investing option among mid-size Italian food companies where the 'art' of preservation of Italian entrepreneurship and roots in gastronomy tradition count a lot.

Protection of mineral water and biodiversity is the most important commitment for the company together with the reduction and recycling of plastic and paper package consumption, especially in relation to plastic (PET included in the pre-forms and HDPE in bottle caps).

Their strategy today is to grow abroad with the mineral water but at the same time through acquisition and export of other Italian historical food brands. Today, they export to 40 countries including China, Europe, US and Arab countries.

Authenticity, empathy and a clear direction together with consistent communication has created a strong reputation of the corporate brand.

PR has been a part of an integrated campaign which includes advertising to support brand awareness, social activities to include and motivate consumer communities, events to underline and celebrate its commitment to no-profit organisations operating in art preservation, medical research, environment and culture. Media writing for business and finance, trends, art and culture, food and beverage are key stakeholders for the PR campaign which began more than 10 years ago.

Guy Esnouf

Communications Director, nPower. Formerly Corporate Communications Director of Rhone Poulenc Rorer, UK

Case: Remember to Be Human

In 1996, I was Communications Director of French – American drug company Rhone Poulenc Rorer when it settled a US class action lawsuit over HIV contaminated blood products. But what was the reputation management process that led up to that settlement?

The Comms management process was straightforward. We engaged a core group of internal stakeholders and advisors, a few key execs and monitored media closely. What was more difficult was what we said – we may not have been legally liable, but they were still our customers. How can we be human without compromising our legal position? In this situation, many companies clam up or adopt the position suggested by our lawyers that these individuals' cases had no merit.

But that's the language of confrontation and the court. As I explained to the Board, imagine you are in a car driven by a friend when a child steps out into the road and gets run over. Will you be guilty? No. Will you do everything you can do to help and support? Yes, of course.

So, our statement was that 'this was a tragedy that no one could have predicted or prevented.' This set the tone for how we behaved: it was human, recognised the tragedy and reiterated our legal defence.

Too many times companies present themselves as cold because they are afraid of the courts but it is better to present yourself as human, because it's humans who judge us. Those humans are our customers, our stakeholders, our employees and of course, we ourselves are human too.

Pavlína Rieselova

Managing Partner, Ewing Public Relations, Czech Republic

Case: The Czech Doctors' Union

In 2010, 20 years after the fall of the Iron Curtain, Czech hospital doctors still only earned 4.50 Euro/hour and to make a living worked 100 hours of overtime each month. For 20 years, they addressed this calmly and quietly with the government but their grievances fell on deaf ears. In 2010, the Czech Doctor's Union asked us to craft a campaign that would result in a pay increase, improvements to continued education and resolution of overtime. Our strategy was far from calm and quiet: they declared their intension to organise a mass resignation by the end of that year. After 59 cities, 70 hospitals and a six-month road show, 4,000 doctors from 80 different hospitals resigned. Throughout the campaign, the government took a 'we'll see' attitude, and hoped 'common sense' would prevail, but when those resignations arrived, a massive anti-campaign was initiated by the Health Ministry, Prime Minister and President. They created hospital evacuation plans and planted images of dying babies in hopes of bullying doctors into reversing those resignations. But it didn't work. Despite the massive negative public sentiment, with under 24 hours left in their two-month notice period, a MOU was signed guaranteeing reform. For two months, Thank You We're Leaving was debated in every pub, on every street corner and was the number 1 leading news story. Doctors were criticised for holding patients' hostage, but this wasn't a popularity contest. It was about meaningful change for 12,000 hospital doctors and ultimately every single patient they treat.

Andreas Fischer-Appelt

CEO and Co-Founder, fischerAppelt AG, Germany

Case: Merck's State of Curiosity

As part of its '2016 State of Curiosity' report, Merck discovered that only 20% of workers in Germany, China and the USA self-identify as curious. To improve this situation, and promote curiosity as the driving force behind innovations in science and technology, the company started the global #catchcurious initiative.

The core objective was to strengthen Merck's reputation as a vibrant science and technology company among customers, innovation partners and potential employees. Our strategy was to harness the power of an inspirational campaign narrative to empower and activate B2B audiences. Via interactive experiments, influencer content and regular editorial features, we infected audiences with the brand's 'Breakthroughs begin with curiosity' message. We harnessed the reach of participating influencers to raise awareness for the campaign across professional and social networks. Displays, video ads and search drove traffic to the microsite.

A 3D journey self-test, regular articles, infographics and expert interviews completed our offering.

The mixture of scientific data and interactive experiences paid off. In less than five months, the microsite recorded 3.2 million-page views from 1.6 million unique B2B visitors.

Influencer partnerships helped spread our message and campaign content to over 37.4 million contacts worldwide. Self-test participants spent an average 4.5 minutes interacting with the 3D feature – generating over 50,000 curiosity profiles.

With curiosity at the heart of its first-ever brand campaign, science and technology-company Merck started #catchcurious. 'Only the curious have something to find'.

Beth Garcia

CEO, Approach and Juntos (a communications company focused on causes), Brazil

Case: Building Reputation with Purpose

Working for 20 years for the same brand requires creativity and, above all, sensitivity to organise the discourse and the paths over time, according to the demands of society.

The first Rock in Rio happened in Rio de Janeiro in 1985, from the dream of the Brazilian publicist Roberto Medina to increase the showbiz industry in the country. Years later, in 2000, I was invited to participate in the relaunch of this brand, which had been off during a long economic crisis. It was a huge project, and it turned this challenge into the most important client of the small communication agency that I was starting.

Since then, Approach has been responsible for the press relations of all editions of the festival in Brazil and in helping to guide international agencies for editions in Lisbon, Madrid and Las Vegas. We work on brand building, which not only brings together renowned international artists, but has also carried the banner of social and environmental issues before any other company, as a marketing tool. Rock in Rio today is one of the biggest entertainment events in the world.

At the Rio de Janeiro edition in 2017, we had a media record. The PR effort resulted in 23,000 reports and a media return of R$2.6 billion. The reputation of the Rock in Rio brand lies in the solidity of the message and the authenticity of what it delivers to its audience. And we are proud to be a part of it.

Hans Gennerud

CEO, Gullers Grupp, Sweden

Case: How the Swedes Came to Love Chicken

Chicken consumption in Sweden has increased greatly in recent years. We now consume 23 kilos per capita − an increase of 300% since the 1990s. 2017 was the first year Swedes consumed as much chicken as beef.

The poultry industry has suffered from several crises over the years, in particular, the bird flu. In dealing with these, we worked closely with the industry, resulting in Sweden becoming the only European country where consumption of chicken did not decrease because of the bird flu.

However, the Swedish industry had a hard time competing with cheaper, imported chicken. Consumers could not tell the difference between imported and domestic chicken. At the same time, companies communicated in different ways. There was no clear collective power that addressed issues and communicated at a higher level.

In 2006, a quality seal was launched and all products that met the tough quality requirements of The Swedish Poultry Association were marked with it. In the second year of the brand-building campaign, the poultry industry reached an all-time high, with sales increasing by 13% and the brand/ quality seal increasing by 700%, after five years.

Our communication strategy has been standing firm. It is about simplifying – highlighting the most important added values and about clarifying – translating these values into something that the Swedes relate to. This includes a clear call-to-action: "Keep an eye out for the Yellow Bird" slogan. We are constantly working in an integrated way regarding reach, using the same basic messages in our own, earned and purchased channels. In addition to consumers, the target groups are opinion leaders, the public sector as well as trade and wholesale.

Lisa George

Founder and Director, Iris Public Relations DMCC, United Arab Emirates

Case: The Land Art Generator Initiative – Taking a Local Sustainability Initiative Global

The Land Art Generator Initiative was started in the UAE by a husband and wife team, Elizabeth and Robert, who launched the campaign to create a platform for artists, architects and other creatives working with engineers and scientists, to bring forward solutions for sustainable energy infrastructures that enhance the city as works of public art while cleanly powering thousands of homes.

It was a new concept with a very low budget and no major industry support. The challenge was to create public awareness, generate entries and attract sponsors.

I approached business, environment and lifestyle media for feature stories on the renewable energy aspect of the campaign and its benefits to society. There was a great media interest, and soon Robert and Elizabeth were on the media interview circuit.

The highlight of the campaign was that it captured international media attention with Robert interviewed by the *New York Times*. UAE's local radio, TV, newspapers and magazines also did feature stories on the LAGI competition.

Prior to the PR campaign, the competition had attracted no significant entries or any sponsors. It soon got the backing of UAE's renewable energy city Masdar, and the entries started pouring in. Today, LAGI is run on a global scale. Our early support is directly responsible for bringing together thousands of people from over 60 countries now working collaboratively for solutions for sustainable energy infrastructures.

And LAGI's work continues, thanks to supporters who believe in the beauty of a sustainable future, and in the value of the arts to highlight scientific advancements.

Neil Green

Chief Executive, Senate SHJ, New Zealand

Case: Picking up the Pieces After the 2011 Canterbury Earthquakes

At 12.51 p.m. on the 22 February 2011, a magnitude 6.3 earthquake struck Christchurch, killing 185 people including 115 in the CTV building of Canterbury Television that collapsed in seconds.

The Government commissioned an expert panel to investigate what happened and they found the building collapsed because of severe horizontal shaking, brittle columns and the building's asymmetrical layout. Communicating these answers was a mammoth undertaking. We had to balance the very technical information against raw emotion and intense media interest.

Senate SHJ worked with the department and expert panel, ministers and a wide range of agencies to ensure the investigation was seen for what it was: authoritative, thorough and impartial. We also worked with foreign missions and victim support agencies to understand the needs of victims' families from overseas, identify cultural nuances and understand the emotional dimension of the communications task. We had to develop communications in eight different languages.

On 9 February 2012, we held separate confidential briefings for families and for the survivors and former tenants. Media were briefed at a separate venue.

Victims' families, sector stakeholders, other agencies and media praised the report as *very factual and very helpful, an exacting job*. The panel of experts were commended and DBH's chief executive received a standing ovation at the presentation of the reports to families of the deceased. Ministers and other government agencies commended the Department for its sensitive management of the events.

Laura Hastings

Joint Managing Director, Lansons, UK

Case: The Co-operative Bank

Few financial organisations have faced a series of crises as significant as the Co-operative Bank between 2013 and 2017. As the UK's ethical bank, it was the perfect storm of unprecedented financial losses: lurid tabloid headlines around the former 'Crystal Methodist' Chairman, two recapitalisations and a further capital raise and intense regulatory and media scrutiny over a five-year period. Lansons worked alongside the new management team to support the turnaround advising across all external and internal stakeholder engagement.

I'd pull out three key things that made a difference to regaining confidence and retaining customers.

(1) Words: It sounds simple but the nuance of what you say in a crisis and striking the right tone really matters. A strong corporate narrative provided the direction of travel. The language used was realistic and humble. We scrutinised every word, from press statements and social media responses to customer letters to make sure it was fit for purpose for whoever heard or saw it.

(2) Tight risk management: New reputational risks were continuously emerging as the situation unfolded, and our careful analysis and management minimised further reputational damage as the Bank sought to stabilise and subsequently recover.

(3) Meaningful action: Despite the turbulent environment, we ensured that the new management's positive actions were heard clearly — creating a drum beat of 'good news' for customers and colleagues to unite behind.

Successfully navigating a crisis of this scale rests on many things but reputation management mattered fundamentally to secure the organisation's future.

Neil Hedges

*Chairman of Headland, formerly Co-founder of
Fishburn Hedges, UK*

Case: Shell

In 1998, my previous agency Fishburn Hedges was appointed by Shell to plan and implement a fully integrated, reputation-building communications campaign.

At the time, Shell's reputation had suffered badly as a result of its activities in the North Sea and Nigeria.

Although it may seem obvious today, Shell's recognition in 1998 that its response to the situation required a completely fresh approach to communications was way ahead of its time.

The campaign we helped to create moved away from 'telling' to a 'listening and responding' approach to stakeholder engagement.

The tone of the dialogue was humble, acknowledging publicly that Shell did not have all the answers to getting the right balance between, in its own words, profits and principles.

A global programme of activity was implemented, ranging from the organisation of local workshops to encouragement of direct dialogue between the company and its critics to the creation of an interactive website facilitating an online discussion between stakeholders and Shell's management at the highest level.

This new approach to external communications had an equally profound impact on the internal culture of Shell, which became much more outward-facing.

For this reason, the effectiveness of the campaign was far more enduring.

The impact, I would argue, lasts to this day.

Bridget von Holdt

Business Director, Burson-Marsteller, South Africa

Case: 'Telling the Net1 Story'

Burson-Marsteller was appointed in March 2017 to manage the crisis communication media relations on the socio-political issue related to social grants' payments on behalf of Net1 UEPS Technologies, a NASDAQ listed company and its subsidiaries.

The sensitive nature of the issue necessitated the adoption of an interactive, engaging crisis management programme. The aim was to empower Net1 with the necessary tools, response measures and strategic counsel to manage the crisis effectively, and in so doing to manage the reputation of Net1 and its subsidiaries, while safeguarding the interests of investors and shareholders.

This entailed influencing the predominantly negative perceptions among journalists, dispelling misconceptions and developing channels of communication with key investors and society at large. Burson-Marsteller, together with Net1 worked towards promoting transparency, creating open lines of communication and responding to all media inquiries.

The approach was threefold: opening up channels of communications with strategic stakeholders, including journalists, as the priority corrective action; rectifying issues and putting the record straight through media roundtables and media tours to Net1's strategic pay points in regions such as the Eastern Cape, North West and Gauteng.

A recent poll of media indicates that after 18 months, media sentiment has mainly shifted to neutral and in some cases positive. The majority of the journalists polled feel that Net1 has become more available to engage with the public.

Artūras Jonkus
Partner, Agency 1323, Lithuania

Case: Yukos

Between 2001 and 2004, I managed communications activities for Russian oil company Yukos in seven Central and Eastern European countries, including the Baltic states, Poland, Hungary, Slovakia, Croatia and Austria. My overall task was to build the reputation of Yukos as a modern corporation, managed according to international business standards. I was also tasked with facilitating business acquisitions in Lithuania and Slovakia, as well as potential deals in the other markets across Central and Eastern Europe.

Within the region, public opinion about Russian companies was often sceptical and negative; in general, they were not perceived as open and transparent businesses. It took time and effort to prove that this was not the case with Yukos.

To achieve a transformation in public perceptions, Yukos implemented a policy of openness towards the international media, experts and NGOs regarding all issues relating to its business activities. As a result of intensive communications efforts over several years, Yukos gained a reputation as a company committed to openness and transparency, and managed according to accepted international business standards.

During the attacks against Yukos by Russian authorities, and their subsequent takeover of the company, the organisation's reputation for openness and transparency enabled Yukos shareholders to safeguard some of the company's assets outside Russia. The company's established reputation for good business practice also aided Yukos shareholders in litigation against the Russian government regarding its takeover of the company.

Janet Kimandi

Director, Levanter Africa, Kenya

Case: M-KOPA Solar

Nairobi-based M-KOPA established a category-leading reputation as the global leading off grid 'pay-as-you-go' energy provider.

In October 2014, 18 months after commercial launch, M-KOPA was about to connect its 100,000th household.

Amidst low awareness and slowed sales volumes, the company was looking to raise funds within 12 months to drive expansion. Investors showed minimal interest as the pay-as-you-go model in off grid communities was not clearly understood.

By January 2016, Levanter Africa had established M-KOPA as the global leader in off grid pay-as-you-go solar energy with accelerated sales and better understanding of the benefits across entire category.

M-KOPA'S promise to its customers was simple and powerful: for the same cost as what low income, off grid homes were spending on kerosene, M-KOPA was offering a connection to solar power for lights, phone charging and radio.

Our communications focused on the impact of replacing Kerosene with solar with customers telling the story wherever possible. This was transformational. Low-income Kenyans hadn't been put at the heart of a global communications programme for a commercial entity.

Tactics were limited to customer stories in photos and film created in the field and pitched monthly to the media, product placements on local media and a bi-annual investor report to help co-investors communicate on business model.

By January 2016, we achieved over 100 media pieces, M-KOPA won the 2015 Zayed Future Energy Prize, listed among the 2015 Global Cleantech 100 and was among Fortune Magazine top 50 companies changing the world. M-KOPA had connected over 300,000 households and raised more than US$40 million. And it transformed over 1.5 million people's lives with clean, affordable power.

Urs Knapp

Partner, Farner Consulting AG, Switzerland

Case: Positioning Johnson & Johnsons' Footprint in Switzerland

J&J is the world's leading healthcare company. In Switzerland, all sectors including Pharmaceutical, Medical Devices, Consumer Health Care have an important presence. The number of jobs generated in Switzerland has tripled in the last 15 years to around 6,600.

J&J has a strong footprint in Switzerland, but isn't as known as it should be as a partner to the society and an employer. Therefore, the Swiss Leadership Team launched a reputation programme in 2015.

Objectives:

- Enhancing the reputation of the brand and the awareness of the businesses.

- Positioning J&J as a relevant partner of the Swiss community.

- Increasing reputation as an attractive employer.

Since its launch in 2015, Farner Consulting has supported the reputation programme with its conceptual, advisory and executive services.

Strategy:

- Building a strong content base for internal and external communications, aligned with corporate content.

- Defining effective communication structures for cross-sector communications activities.

- Thinking as one brand — but acting locally with specific measures for sites and sectors.

Selected measures:

- A comprehensive 100-page-presentation, 'Together for a healthy Switzerland', in four languages.

- An engagement programme with key stakeholders.

- Specific content for different channels, offline and online, for example:
  - Factsheets for defined internal and external stakeholders.

  - Media roundtable and other media activities.

  - Corporate video.

  - Intranet and Internet.

First results (the programme is still ongoing):

There has been a measurable rise in reputation and attention for J&J in Switzerland.

Luke Lambert

President and CEO, G&S Business Communications, USA

Case: Celebrating Women in Agriculture

Taking the position that reputation management can be a proactive discipline, G&S Business Communications worked with Syngenta, a global agricultural leader, to elevate brand affinity in the US, where loyalty to specific Syngenta brands can eclipse feelings about the company itself.

Syngenta wanted to transcend reputations of its individual products and build broader brand affinity. Doing so would require tapping into an emotive driver with universal application across the US farming industry, from California almond growers to Idaho potato growers. The G&S recommendation:

align with the relatively unsung but strong force of women in agriculture.

Fact: Women account for 30% of all US farmers. In 2016, G&S advised Syngenta to join the burgeoning 'FarmHer' movement by sponsoring an inaugural TV series dedicated to 'shining a light on women of agriculture'.

To amplify Syngenta's celebration of women in agriculture, G&S developed an integrated multi-media campaign including 30-second featurettes of women in agriculture, TV episodes featuring female Syngenta employees, media relations, sponsored and earned social media, participation in agriculture community and internal events.

Through FarmHer, Syngenta developed an emotive connection to the broader farm community. The inaugural campaign earned 237,842,830 potential impressions, far exceeding expectations. The campaign reached a vast audience of potential brand loyalists and engaged with current and potential customers. Post-campaign research revealed that in 2016, the Non-Customers Affinity Index for Syngenta increased by 7%. For non-customers, willingness to purchase rose 1.3% and willingness to try a new product rose 2.8%.

David Liu, (BJG-WSW)

Chairman (China), Weber Shandwick, China

Case: The Beijing Olympics

Having the honour of assisting Beijing in its winning bid for the 2008 and 2022 Olympics were two of the proudest moments of my career at Weber Shandwick. It was an enormous privilege to work alongside a team of experts from the bidding committee to secure China's place in history as the first city to host the Summer and Winter Games.

The focal point of both campaigns was markedly different as were the challenges.

In the case of the 2008 Games, which was to be China's 'launch' party, the emphasis was on China's economic developments. At this stage, hundreds of millions of people had been lifted out of poverty. Several years later, we found ourselves knuckled down in the war room again with the bidding committee as everyone prepared to help Beijing complete the 'double whammy'. This time, the message was that Beijing was the economic and sustainable choice as the capital had Olympic-ready existing infrastructure that could be re-used.

However, there was a persistent media perception of Beijing as a city that lacked natural snow and a winter sports culture.

Op-eds, international social media posts and press conferences were organised to put forward Beijing's side of the story. There was a 24/7 media office. Celebrities such as actor Jackie Chan and basketball sensation Yao Ming were engaged in the campaign to shed some star power. As a result, Beijing won again.

Everyone worked incredibly hard for both victories. Although these were challenging times, the memories are unforgettable.

Rebecca Mayo

Joint Managing Director, Lansons, UK

Case: moneysupermarket.com

It's a privilege to look back on your career and realise you played a part in a phenomenon, a consumer finance phenomenon that triggered a seismic shift in British retail financial services. Did we predict the almost revolutionary impact Simon Nixon and his price comparison website moneysupermarket.com would have? Perhaps not fully. But we did work alongside the team to build one of the most influential reputations in the industry, from its launch in 1999 to its £840 million float in 2007.

In my experience, working with start-ups and fast-growing organisations requires a different mindset. You're responsible for continually considering the business from different perspectives — its flaws, its potential and its future. For building (and managing) a reputation from scratch, with the same degree of ambition as the entrepreneur behind it. It was this that led Ian Williams, then Lansons Joint MD, to suggest naming the business moneysupermarket.com. It was a critical decision. It meant consumers and influencers could grasp the new concept of price comparison almost immediately.

Working with Simon and the team, we then created a reputation and influence building strategy that endures today, nearly 20 years later. We positioned moneysupermarket.com at the heart of a revolution 'levelling the playing field, dispelling confusion and empowering consumers to take control'. A team of moneysupermarket.com commentators worked relentlessly for nearly a decade to advise consumers how to make the most of their money and switch products, often by exposing poor practice and bad deals in every sector. This not only led to an unrivalled industry profile, but it engaged consumers and attracted providers, creating a circle of credibility and influence that helped strengthen moneysupermarket.com's reputation and business model at a pivotal time in its corporate history.

Nicola Nel

*Managing Director and Client Lead, Atmosphere
Communications, South Africa*

Case: Capitec Bank

In February 2018, Capitec Bank, one of South Africa's biggest banks, came under attack. Rogue short sellers in New York exploited the naivety of local analysts and investors by creating havoc in the local stock market. A research house, Viceroy Research, employed a 'short and distort approach' – shorting a share and releasing a damning report full of inaccurate accusations – which sent Capitec's share price into freefall, dropping by more than 30% overnight.

Panic ensued from investors, regulators and the bank's clients. The risk was immense and if not immediately addressed would result in a 'run' on the bank, risking not only a collapse, but damaging the trust in South Africa's banking industry and the country's economy.

We implemented a high-impact crisis communications plan to restore calm in markets and client trust, stabilising the bank's share price and securing clients' deposits. Our fast-paced approach included responding to client and investor concerns immediately, by convincing Capitec to communicate proactively, regularly and transparently.

We held a press conference within hours, arranged media interviews, facilitated a global telecom with investors, issued media statements and executed investor communications. We seeded endorsements from credible analysts and academics, rallied support from regulators, including the treasury, industry players, clients and social influencers using earned media, owned platforms, social media and direct communications.

After a tumultuous two weeks, Capitec Bank emerged with its reputation intact and was hailed for its outstanding management of the crisis. Within a month, its share price returned to pre-Viceroy levels and its stock gained the most in two years.

Manash K Neog and Sugandha Mahajan

Manager Co-Founder and Director; Manager – Public Policy (respectively), Chase India, India

Case: Championing Sustainable Antibiotics

DSM Sinochem Pharmaceuticals (DSP) is a global leader in the sustainable production of antibiotics and actively advocates on the issue of Antimicrobial Resistance (AMR). However, when we initiated our policy advocacy campaign for them in India in 2016, there was little awareness among stakeholders about AMR and the need for sustainability in the antibiotic supply chain.

We shared policy papers and our recommendations with key stakeholders at the Prime Minister's Office and other Government departments in one-to-one meetings. We urged them to initiate action to contain AMR, which globally results in over 700,000 deaths a year. Following our meetings, the Prime Minister spoke about AMR in his radio show 'Mann ki Baat', and other Government departments started looking at AMR as a public health challenge. Based on DSP's Dutch expertise, we recommended a 'one-health' approach to tackle AMR, which would ensure multi-stakeholder involvement. Subsequently, the National Action Plan on AMR was launched based on the one-health approach in April 2017.

To showcase DSP's manufacturing clean practices, a study tour to DSP's plant was arranged for Central Pollution Control Board (CPCB), National Centre for Disease Control teams (NCDC) and Department of Biotechnology. Subsequently, DSP was selected as one of the members of

CPCB's Expert Group to draft standards for antibiotic residue in industrial effluent.

Through ongoing engagement with non-government stakeholders like the WHO and civil societies, participation in key conferences and regular educational workshops for industry (STEM), we have been able to establish DSP as leader in sustainable antibiotics and AMR containment in India. In April 2018, the State Government of Kerala also invited DSP for their workshop on AMR containment and antibiotic sustainability.

Kristina Nikolayeva

Managing Director, Be-It Agency, Ukraine

Case: The Coca-Cola Company Ukraine

In 2016, Be-it Agency helped the Coca-Cola Company in Ukraine not only to mitigate a reputational crisis and risk of business being banned from a successful 40 million + consumer market, but also to strengthen reputation, elevate trust and brand love.

The crisis exploded, when Coca-Cola Russia's agency published a map of the Russian Federation, including the territory of Ukraine – an illegally occupied Crimea, on the company's website and social media. It caused huge damage to Coca-Cola's reputation in Ukraine, as the situation quickly escalated to the top political news, because of the hot context. Moreover, several high-level opinion leaders called to boycott the company and its products.

For years, Coca-Cola Ukraine invested a lot in community development. So, our idea was to rebuild the reputation on what the company had already done in Ukraine and the established relations. We engaged partner opinion leaders to defend the company in social and traditional media. This changed the tonality of the narrative from negative to neutral or positive. Then we filmed and promoted two videos about Coca-Cola's economic and social value for Ukraine, with employees, partners and beneficiaries of company's projects instead of actors.

By the end of 2016, the corporate reputation index grew by 17% and became the highest one compared to the other international market peers (GfK Corporate Reputation Survey). Trust to the company and brand love significantly increased: 74% Ukrainians agreed that 'Coca-Cola is an example of business practice for others'.

Arturo Pinedo

Partner and General Manager, Llorente y Cuenca, Spain

Case: Campofrío — Keeping a Promise Alive

Campofrío is one of the largest companies in the processed meats sector, present in eight European countries. In November 2014, the company's main factory in Burgos burned down. Prior to the fire, Campofrío's overall communication strategy was barely developed, and thus the challenge was to turn a crisis into an opportunity to relaunch the Campofrío brand in Spain, through overcoming either the risks caused by the destruction of jobs, the suspicion about rebuilding the plant or the lack of a clear corporate positioning of the company. Between 2015 and 2016, a plan based on four pillars — commitment, credibility, risk management and governmental support — was established.

The most relevant milestones of this process were the signing of an agreement between Campofrío and its employees for the start-up of the new factory in Burgos, the 'event of the Reincorporation', when all employees were called to a meeting where their contracts were reactivated, and the visit of the

Spanish Prime Minister to the plant, and later the presence of the King of Spain on the official grand opening.

These events and PR campaigns achieved widespread media coverage, with more than 1,300 news about the new factory, an estimated audience of more than 528 million readers and an economic value of 7.5 million euros throughout its two years. The objective of recovering the company's reputation was fully met: according to Rep Track Spain 2016, Campofrío held the 22nd position in the ranking and got the best employee evaluation in that year.

Eliza Rogalski

Founder, Rogalski Damaschin Public Relations, Romania

Case: There Is No Better Way to Consolidate Public Trust Than a Crisis

Since 2005, Romania has faced the challenge of Avian Influenza, which has caused widespread panic across the country. Alongside topics from the international press, news about cases of avian flu were continuously detected throughout Romania, causing the story to be kept on the front pages.

Due to the lack of knowledge about virus spreading, Romanians have become reluctant to consume chicken, and business partners have interrupted or renegotiated contracts with the producers. The entire indigenous industry has been disturbed and imports of poultry meat have increased, even though these foods are not of greater safety. Against this background, Agricola Bacău, the leader of the Romanian chicken market and one of the main exporters in the country, experienced a decrease in sales volumes, common across the entire industry.

But the company did not wait for better times to come. They asked for a communication programme that not only explained to people why their products were safe from bird flu but also consolidated the overall reputation while creating a platform that could prevent any similar future situations.

We created a strategy based on two anchors: the creation of a 'trust-mark' for Agricola Bacău, which would support the whole product portfolio and the communication of the sanitary-veterinary arguments that would entitle the company to take this unique public approach. This 'trust-mark' was called 'BIOSECURIZED', and was a logo applied on all the chicken products of the company. This was communicated with an integrated campaign featuring employees explaining why 'Bio-secured' means 'safe'. By next quarter, Agricola became the number one voice explaining the principles of safe food and the benefits of Bio-secured.

After four months of campaigning, sales increased by 13%. Two months later, the mechanism of our campaign inspired other industries such as bakery to also create trust-marks and communicate high quality, safe food products. The company came out stronger and demonstrated that a crisis is the best moment to confirm values, generate loyalty and inspire.

Doy Roque

Founder and Managing Director, M2.0 Communications, Philippines

Case: Changing the Course of Election History in the Philippines

In 2009, M2.0 was approached by a Venezuelan technology firm with one ask: turn the company's tarnished reputation from garbage to gold.

Smartmatic, a company that made election machines, had won the government tender to automate the coming presidential election. The upstart firm had a massive task: automate elections for over 50 million people in less than 12 months.

Hard as it already was, this job had become fraught with risks from accusations of corruption and suggestions of vote-rigging.

It became clear from the outset that M2.0's job was to get the media off of Smartmatic's back. Here, the agency saw an opportunity in utilising Smartmatic's top human asset: its young and charismatic President, Cesar Flores.

M2.0 lost no time in placing Flores in the spotlight, making sure that he had weekly press conferences with politicians and election officials. Flores engaged the press vigorously, with full transparency becoming a clear message. The campaign eventually leveraged the concept of cognitive dissonance: How could such an endearing young executive lead such an 'evil' company? People had to resolve that conflict emotionally, and with that the public started to align perception along a more palatable question: maybe we should give Smartmatic an even chance?

After the 2010 elections, Smartmatic became a media darling for pulling off the Philippines' first-ever automated national elections. Not a bad job for a once-reviled company that ended up changing the course of a country's history.

Prema Sagar

Vice Chair, Burson-Marsteller Asia Pacific and Principal and Founder, Genesis Burson-Marsteller, India

Case: Bringing Back Nestlé Maggi Noodles from crisis

Operating in India since 1912, Nestlé, the world's largest processed foods company, is a household name in the country, whether for its iconic coffee, Nescafé or its flagship Maggi Noodles. In June 2015, Nestlé faced an existential threat when the foods regulatory authority, FSSAI, accused it of selling spurious Maggi Noodles based on test reports from various state-run labs. Nestlé decided to voluntarily withdraw over

32,000 tonnes of Maggi Noodles. FSSAI also banned its manufacture and sale across the country. The net sales for the year 2015 was approximately INR 81.23 billion (US$1.19 billion), which was a drop from the previous year. It was unquestionably the worst conflict in the Swiss company's 150-year history.

Genesis Burson-Marsteller was tasked with helping the brand fight the ban and the negative perception, win back consumer trust and rebuild its brand value. The firm's strategy was to reverse Nestlé's approach of selective contact with the media, replacing it with proactive engagement and support in preparing impactful messaging to energise employees, partners and consumers to become Nestlé's advocates and supporters.

There was a turnaround in media, and subsequently the consumer and market sentiment. Consumer trust on the brand was pegged at 89%. Maggi Noodles relaunched in a record time of less than two months after the Bombay High Court overthrew the FSSAI's ban in August 2015 and allowed resumption of manufacturing and sale.

Jean-Leopold Schuybroek

Founder and Honorary Chairman, Interel, Belgium

Case: D'Ieteren and the Volkswagen Emissions Scandal

When the Volkswagen emissions scandal broke in September 2015, D'Ieteren, the exclusive distributor of Volkswagen vehicles in Belgium, called Interel to avoid being dragged into what would become one of the biggest corporate crises in recent history.

With some 300,000 customers in Belgium owning affected vehicles, there was an urgent need to restore confidence quickly.

The local press was interpreting the situation and raising the temperature of the scandal. Politicians immediately reacted negatively. Car dealers found themselves dealing with worried customers and a potential impact on sales.

A customer care website was set up, enabling D'Ieteren to keep control over the communication through one single channel, limiting negative impact on social media and maintaining consistency of message. This also contributed to reduce the pressure on the car dealer network.

Regular updates were provided to the media, while ensuring 24/7 availability of spokespeople. Well-balanced media coverage was obtained and contributed to the reduction of consumer and political concern.

Meetings were organised with all relevant government officials and D'Ieteren's CEO was prepared for hearings in parliament, with his recommendations being retained in the final parliamentary reports.

In order to protect the car brands from reputation damage, the D'Ieteren brand was put forward in all communications. Key measurement indicators were the absence of impact on D'Ieteren's share price and market share.

'Constant anticipation, permanent availability, fully dedicated advisors, well-thought out communication strategy, easy access to key stakeholders: this is a non-exhaustive overview of the added value provided by Interel', D'Ieteren Auto's CEO concluded.

Kevin Soady
Partner, Kekst CNC, UK

Case: Bayer

When planning a major corporate transaction, advisers have always worked with clients to deeply scrutinise issues in order to understand their relevance and impact. The growth in online conversations and the emergence of influencer networks have transformed this element of transactional planning. It is now often critical that advisers make the best use of detailed analytics and mapping of online influencers, complementing traditional networks.

Clients and bankers increasingly recognise that some of the loudest voices commenting on and criticising a transaction can never be swayed from an entrenched position. But that does not mean that these people and their views should be ignored.

Increasingly we need to monitor, categorise and then patrol the borders. Being prepared to hit back hard when malevolent challenges to a firm's reputation, raised innocently or deliberately, look set to cross into the mainstream. This means spending time working proactively to challenge poorly conceived concepts and deliberate misinformation through facts and substance. And increasingly there is a need to stand up to scrutiny both online and in-person.

When my client, Bayer, announced that it would take over Monsanto in 2016, it knew it would have to work hard to maintain trust and reputation. That Bayer has been able to preserve trust in its brand and enhance its reputation with mainstream audiences, reinforces the power of relationships, issues analysis and open-engagement.

Ralph Sutton

International Managing Partner, Avenir Global, UK

Case: Global Salmon Initiative (GSI)

Despite increased demand for its product, the salmon farming industry faces many barriers to expansion due to its negative reputation among consumers and regulators.

In 2011, I participated in a meeting with a small group of CEOs of salmon farming companies from Norway, Chile and Scotland focused on reputation and sustainability. We arranged a speaker from the Canadian forest industries who told the story of their experience leading that industry through a process of engagement, and ultimately successful collaboration with the environmental NGOs based on a mutual commitment to solving problems.

The impact of this discussion was immediate. The group connected with other CEOs and early in 2013 established the Global Salmon Initiative (GSI), a CEO-led initiative focused on driving sustainability across the salmon industry. Since then GSI has delivered on this goal through four pillars of (1) pre-competitive cooperation within the industry around improving practices on sustainability, (2) authentic partnerships with stakeholders including those who have criticised the industry and (3) transparent reporting of progress and communications to explain what GSI members are doing to improve sustainability. The level of transparency, as symbolised by GSI's sustainability report (https://globalsalmoninitiative.org/en/sustainability-report/protein-production-facts) has won praise from different NGOs.

The result has been a powerful collaboration between industry, NGOs and other stakeholders to improve sustainability, grow social licence and improve reputation among key stakeholders. Groups like WWF now point to GSI as a model for how other industries can operate.

Ultimately, what makes this work is the genuine, top-down commitment of the CEOs to industry change.

Henning Sverdrup
Founding Partner, Släger, Norway

Case: SOS Children's Villages

In early 2014, that I was asked by SOS Children's Villages, to create a fundraiser campaign to help keep the freezing children of Syria warm during winter. SOS

Children's Villages was positioned as a humanitarian organisation that provided long-term care for children in need.

Our task was to convince the Norwegian population that the humanitarian crisis in Syria required our full attention, and required concrete actions, that is — funding of immediate on-the-ground project carried out by SOS Childrens Villages. Our challenge was that there were already three organisations in the market addressing the same issue, with solid reputation as emergency aid organisations — which we lacked.

The campaign 'Little Boy Freezing', the little boy at the bus stop with no coat on, hit a global nerve. It was the first hidden camera social experiment that went viral. Approximately 138 million people saw the whole campaign and it was on the news across the world, generating an enormous momentum.

Most importantly the campaign kept 26,000 children warm that winter, and also ended up creating far more awareness.

Släger's campaign, *Little Boy Freezing* not only elevated SOS Children's Villages brand and reputation globally, but also help improve its reputation, as an organisation with the capabilities and structure to successfully carry out emergency aid operations.

Daniel Tisch

CEO, Argyle Public Relations, Canada

Case: The American Peanut Council

In 2009, salmonella-contaminated peanut butter at a Georgia plant was linked to nine deaths and 691 illnesses across North America — and a recall of some 4,000 products, with an estimated $1 billion cost. Within days, Argyle was managing the US peanut industry's communications during the largest food recall in North American history.

Argyle's insights: To protect the industry's reputation – and reverse a massive decline in sales – we had to exceed public expectations, build up the client's communications capacity, become a leading online source for consumers and aggressively align the industry with the public interest.

During a recall, companies and industries often say they are 'cooperating' with the investigation. We went much further, launching one of the first large-scale social/digital crisis programmes, targeting Google search to drive visits to our site. As regulators issued daily lists of affected products, we gave consumers a list of products confirmed safe.

To protect confidence in the industry, we had a leading independent microbiologist speak to the media about the industry's safety record, while a top nutritionist provided accessible advice to parents. This turned the extensive media coverage from highly negative and inaccurate to balanced and accurate.

Finally, anticipating public scrutiny of the industry, Argyle facilitated an industry summit that achieved a consensus to review its agricultural and manufacturing practices. The result: a rapid recovery in consumer trust and consumption. By the end of 2009, the industry achieved record sales, and our programme earned the highest national and global PR awards in 2010.

Richard Tsang

Chairman, Strategic Public Relations Group, Hong Kong

Case: Shue Yan College

Dr. Chung Chi-yung co-founded Shue Yan College in 1971, which became Hong Kong's first private university in

2006 in response to immense competition faced by students seeking university enrolment. Her passing in 2014 was a major blow to the institution. Overshadowed by well-funded public universities and impacted by a declining youth population, Shue Yan saw enrolment drop in recent years.

To turn the tide, a comprehensive publicity campaign was developed by SPRG in late 2016 to rejuvenate Shue Yan's image to attract a new generation of students. A two-pronged strategy was devised, which involved raising the profile of the institution and maximising peer-group influence. Correspondingly, the University's website adopted a simplified, user-friendly format to appeal to today's young audience. Furthermore, the dedicated website of its renowned Department of Journalism and Communication took on the appearance of a digital news network so that the website and students could gain a higher level of exposure. Also, leveraging SPRG's ties with the media, special columns were created featuring contributions from Shue Yan professors.

Capitalising on the power of social media, students representing all 12 academic programmes were featured in Facebook and selected websites to disseminate their positive experiences. Traditional media was also employed, with interviews that helped turn the spotlight on Shue Yan students' various achievements, thus further bolstering the University's image.

While the majority of private post-secondary institutions experienced a decline in enrolment in 2017, Shue Yan was a rare exception, achieving a significant year-on-year increase of 40%.

Marilú de la Luz Velasco

Executive Vice President, Extend, Chile

Case: Rebuilding a Shaken Image

For Chile, a country constantly hit by natural disasters, the National Emergency Office (Onemi) constitutes a vital entity. The confidence in its alertness and capabilities is the difference between life and death.

After the 8.8 magnitude earthquake in 2010, which led to deaths and missing people, Onemi's reputation collapsed and for years, it was struck by multiple political and legal accusations.

In January 2015, we took on the challenge of rebuilding this discredited institution's credibility and confidence. At the time Onemi only had 31%[17] citizen approval. Joining together with Onemi's new management in their efforts, we built a communications strategy to position it as a proactive institution focusing on making all Onemi´s initiatives visible.

The main objective was to educate. Through an emotional, didactic and simple narrative, we engaged citizens in understanding safety protocols and taking a preventive role in their own safety. In addition to general messages, we created separate messages and materials for three different audiences: early adopters, pointing out that the security is their responsibility, people affected by natural disasters, with guidelines in emergencies, and influencers which directly impact Onemi's image and duty, explaining the coordination's role of Onemi in natural disasters.

Working daily with all communication tools, we turned every new disaster in opportunities to expose Onemi's new competences.

In April 2018, the latest public survey showed that Onemi has a 66%[18] citizen approval. These results directly impact the population, increasing the chances they may act correctly facing a future natural catastrophe.

Uwe Wache

Managing Partner, Klenk & Hoursch AG, Germany

Case: Aegis Media

In October 2006, Klenk & Hoursch AG was commissioned by Aegis Media for a consulting mandate, shortly before an anonymous charge had been filed against its then acting CEO, led to his arrest. The accusation was of embezzlement of Aegis Media funds. Over the years, millions of Euros of client money had gone into the CEO's pockets. The criminal proceedings attracted a great deal of media attention at a national level in Germany. During the course of court proceedings, the CEO of Aegis Media was accused of complicity and systemic fraud against its clients. Therefore, due to the complexity of the matter, the company was exposed to negative publicity for a long time, with corresponding negative effects on its reputation. Important client segments became unstable and threatened to break away. In this critical phase for the company, it was crucial to ensure that both the legal and communication strategies were consistently coordinated to point out the CEO's individual misconduct and to reassure existing clients all of which was achieved successfully. The 'scandal' in media reporting over time was linked with the name of the CEO and not the company name. After 16 months of court proceedings, the CEO was finally confirmed guilty by the court. In May 2009, he was sentenced to 11 years and three months in prison for embezzlement in 68 cases. This ended a long phase of uncertainty for the company and restored its reputation.

Scott Widmeyer

Founder and Chairman, Widmeyer Communications (now a Finn Partners company), USA

Case: Whittle Communications: Channel One News

When it comes to how to run US public education, everyone has an opinion, and it's important to listen. Our client at the time was Whittle Communications who was on the cusp of piloting a first-of-its-kind TV news programme for American classrooms.

However, the folks behind *Channel One News* did not get the message about doing all of their homework (no pun intended!). Opposition was building from the education establishment, including teacher unions, who felt TV news wrapped up with advertising had no place in the classroom.

I believed strongly that US teens could benefit from a 12-minute daily news programme — even with a little bit of advertising. In fact, our schools are surrounded by advertising from book covers to stadium signage and more.

We happily went to work on Whittle's behalf and quickly changed the equation. My initial effort was to help the editorial writer of the *New York Times* weigh the pros and cons of Channel One and not take a negative stand on the roll-out of the pilot in four US school districts. With that accomplished, Widmeyer then got engaged in working with influential educators to quell the uprising. We did this through effective communications, giving them a role as advisors around content and creating programming helpful to their own professional development.

The most significant result came when the highly respected president of the American Federation of Teachers (the late Albert Shanker) rethought his opposition and opened the door for Channel One to enter US schools and reach up to 10 million junior and senior high school students.

While Channel One continued to have adversaries, acceptance increased over the years to the point where then President Bill Clinton used Channel One airwaves to address high school students around the country following the horrific Columbine school shootings.

It's always gratifying to reflect on the contributions we can make to supporting a client, and especially when the client is doing the right thing.

Ian Wright, CBE

Chief Executive, Food and Drink Federation, formerly Corporate Relations Director, Diageo (2000–2014), UK

Case: Making a Difference

In the Spring of 2000 Diageo, the recently created combination of Guinness and GrandMet was still recovering from the scandals associated with Ernest Saunders of Guinness and the racy past of GrandMet's Maxwell Joseph.

Emerging from that past was the most serious legacy issue: the fate of the victims of thalidomide[19] – the most notorious drug failure in history. Diageo, of course, had never had anything to do with the drug (or any pharmaceuticals). Yet the long chain of M&A which culminated in its creation had included the acquisition of the business which had sold thalidomide under licence in the UK and the Commonwealth.

Diageo's new leaders wanted to know what to do. Simultaneously, there was the possibility of legal class action from alleged victims of alcohol. So, the natural reaction was to 'repel all borders'. Yet with my team – and our legal colleagues – we saw a different opportunity. If we did the right thing by those impacted by thalidomide, the issue might define how stakeholders thought about Diageo and establish the business credentials for behaving appropriately on the issue of responsible alcohol.

We negotiated with thalidomide victims. It was long and detailed and fraught. We sought to balance the obvious financial needs of those impacted — and their entirely justified emotional need for someone to take responsibility — with the fact that we, as a business, genuinely had no involvement in the tragedy. After nearly two years of negotiation, we reached a settlement. For the first time in nearly 40 years, the victims of thalidomide had agreed a settling rather than having one imposed on them.

My Chairman, James Blyth and I were able to meet a large number of the UK victims at an event they organised. We apologised for what had happened to them and the fact that it had taken so long to reach an amicable agreement. Nearly a decade later, I would have the chance to do the same in Australia. Ever since, even though they have vigorously pursued those who invented the drug and who denied culpability for its shameful legacy, UK thalidomide victims have generously recognised that Diageo has done its best to help.

It will never be enough to compensate those who have suffered so badly. But it set a tone in Diageo for the following decade. It would be a business which would negotiate hard but would do the right thing. It is no co-incidence that responsible drinking emerged as a concept at the same time and that it has transformed the debate about alcohol consumption.

Doing the right thing does not mean giving in. It means recognising what the circumstances and common-sense demand for the reputation and overall good of the organisation. It is the very definition of good business.

10

CRISIS MANAGEMENT

When I told people that I was writing a book about reputation management, roughly four in five of them assumed that the book was about crisis management. And the two separate but related disciplines of crisis management and crisis communication have become specialisms in their own right, hence a separate chapter in this book.

We see many more corporate crises than we used to. McKinsey calculates that there were eight times as many headlines signalling corporate reputation risk at a Fortune Top 100 company, between 2010 and 2016 as there were between 1990 and 1999 (Kalavar and Mysore, 2017) and 64% of senior executives believe that the world has become a riskier place to do business, according to research by the Economist Intelligence Unit (FTI, 2017).

The costs of crises are greater too. McKinsey calculates that major penalties paid by US corporations for regulatory infractions were five times greater in 2015 than in 2010. And that figure takes no account of share price decline or reputational damage.

The increased frequency of crises makes it inevitable that all CEOs and CCOs will endure a crisis at some point in their career. As will virtually all organisations over a 20 (or maybe even 10) year period.

MITIGATING RISK NOT ELIMINATING RISK

In the modern world risk cannot be eliminated, (particularly cyber security risk) it can only be mitigated and managed. As UK business leader and politician Dido Harding says in her excellent 'crisis tips' on pages 189–190, Boards shouldn't be asking 'are we safe?' (because the answer is 'no') but 'where are we vulnerable?' and 'what are we doing to mitigate those risks?'

We find that many organisations are not joined up in their approach to crisis preparedness. Legal requirements around the world require organisations to compile risk registers either for their regulator, for their investors or both. Sometimes these registers are compiled without considering broader societal risks. On other occasions, risks appear on the risk register, but are not included in ongoing risk mitigation or crisis preparedness exercises. The answer, as in all areas of reputation management, is fewer siloes and a more integrated approach.

THE CRISIS PLAYBOOK

Crisis preparedness is essential for all organisations. The latest buzzword in our business is the 'playbook', although if you're from the 1970s you can still say 'manual'.

The playbook matters because having agreed protocols and rehearsed behaviours is essential when the crisis hits. We find that organisational preparedness has improved massively in recent years, particularly incident management protocols and escalation processes. As I said in Chapter 5, in a crisis, organisations insist on the most efficient structure to get the job done.

The most common gaps that we see in crisis preparedness are in rehearsal and updating of protocols, and there often isn't enough testing of whether all of the planned communications processes actually work.

MOST ORGANISATIONS RECOVER

In the midst of the crisis itself, solace is to be found in the fact that, nowadays, most organisations that suffer crises do, eventually recover. Some recover very quickly. Samsung is a good example of this, going from exploding phones in 2016 to 'stellar performance' in 2017 (Jung-a, 2018).

There is very clear logic behind the statement that most organisations recover reputation. We talk all the time about how social media storms engulf organisations so quickly. But just as quickly, they are gone, engulfing someone else. And quite often forgotten.

And as there are eight times as many publicly known corporate crises than there were in the 1990s, they individually must have less impact than they once did. Particularly as we are all suffering from information overload.

There are two types of situation where organisations don't recover relatively quickly from crisis.

The first is where the cause of the crisis, the wrongdoing, is so unacceptable that recovery is impossible. Harvey Weinstein will never recover reputation. Bell Pottinger and Cambridge Analytica were killed by their crises.

Good crisis management is the key to reputational recovery. The second situation that makes recovery difficult is where the crisis is badly managed.

GOOD CRISIS MANAGEMENT IS THE KEY TO REPUTATIONAL RECOVERY

The many corporate crises that we've long forgotten were probably handled well. They fixed the problem and they communicated clearly and accurately. As international banker Niall Booker says, 'reputation is critical and can be managed'[20]. In the crises that are most easily remembered, we often remember the crisis management mistakes more than the cause of the crisis in the first place.

Recovering the operational situation in a crisis takes as long as it takes. It took BP 87 days to cap the oil spill in the Gulf of Mexico. What many people remember, however, is that CEO Tony Hayward, in the midst of the crisis, said 'I'd like my life back' (Durando, 2010). By this point, BP had long since lost any sympathy it may have had from the American people. As bestselling crisis management author Steven Fink says, 'never lose sight of the fact that in the pitched battle between perception and reality, perception *always* wins.'[21]

Too often, the first response to a clear problem is to deny it. Facebook's reputational decline has been at least in part due to the years it has spent claiming videos that have been flagged to 'moderators' as offensive, don't breach its 'community standards'. In 2018, Oxfam CEO Mark Goldring tried to publicly justify hiding the full facts from the public as it would have damaged fundraising, as Hazel Westwood points out in her excellent case study at the end of this chapter.

Making the right big calls during a crisis is crucial. Honesty, accuracy and transparency in communication are key. To Dido Harding, 'in times of existential threat, the CEO is the reputation manager with the responsibility to tell customers and other stakeholders what's happening'. She adds that 'if things go wrong and you fess up early and then put it right, you're always better off in the end'.

The worst thing to do is to cover up the initial crisis or mistake. The cover up invariably causes more damage than the crisis would have done by itself. This seems to be where the long VW 'emissions scandal' is heading. From Watergate onwards, cover-ups have brought down more leaders than crises.

This chapter is completed by: crisis tips from UK business leader and politician, Dido Harding; my interview with 'global troubleshooter' Niall Booker and Hazel Westwood's case study of the Oxfam scandal of 2018.

Tips for Managing a Crisis

Interview with Dido Harding

Business Leader and Politician

Diana Dido Harding, Baroness Harding of Winscombe, is one of the most experienced and high-profile women business leaders in the United Kingdom. She is currently Chair of National Health Service (NHS) Improvement and a non-executive director on the Bank of England's Court of Directors and Chair of the Bank's Remuneration Committee. She sits in the House of Lords as a Conservative peer and is a member of the Economic Affairs Select Committee. She has held executive leadership positions at Tesco, Sainsbury, Kingfisher and Thomas Cook — and was for seven years Chief Executive of leading UK telecom provider TalkTalk Group (TalkTalk). In 1998 a horse she had bought to ride herself, Cool Dawn, won the Cheltenham Gold Cup, Britain's premier steeplechase, as documented in her book, Cool Dawn: My National Velvet *(1999).*

I asked for her for tips on crisis management:

- *In times of existential threat, the CEO is the reputation manager with the responsibility to tell customers and other stakeholders what's happening.*

- *Follow your instincts, don't always listen to 'the talking heads'.*

- *We need to talk openly about the cyber security threat. If we make it a taboo, the criminals win.*

- *Sometimes, the best way to protect customers is to warn them, even if you don't know all of the details.*

- *If the organisation has made a mistake it should say sorry, and while you have to talk to the lawyers about how to say sorry, the reputational hit from not apologising is often much bigger than the legal liability from apologising.*

- *Customers respect authenticity. A CEO that appears quickly on national and social media, being honest and open, even if they look frazzled, is more reassuring than anonymous calm press statements.*

- *The question all Boards should ask their CEOs about cyber is not 'are we safe?' (because the answer is 'no') but 'where are we vulnerable? what are we doing to mitigate those risks?'*

- *If things go wrong and you fess up early and then put it right, you're always better off in the end.*

- *It is possible to turn a crisis into an opportunity to materially improve an organisation. Good crisis management requires non-hierarchical, data-driven decision making and great talent within the organisation rising to the challenge. Boards can be braver and as a result, businesses can emerge better than before.*

THE GLOBAL TROUBLESHOOTER

Interview with Niall Booker

International Banker

In a 30-year career with HSBC, Niall Booker headed the bank's operations in North America, India, Thailand and Dubai before leaving in 2011. Within HSBC he built a reputation as the man to turn to in a crisis and helped unwind the disastrous acquisition of Household in the United States and rebuild the relationship with US regulators following the money laundering issues the bank faced. He was the natural choice to lead the UK's largest mutual bank, The Co-operative Bank, following the £1.5 billion capital shortfall discovered in 2013 and in a four-year stint he led the team that, against the odds, ensured the bank lived to fight another day.

The troubleshooter's fresh pair of eyes invariably find that things are worse than indicated, says Niall, 'you start in an inquisitive mode, ask open questions and find out what you have to fix and be brutally realistic. This doesn't make you popular, but as you will only get one chance it's really important that you make a realistic assessment first time. The first 100 days are about establishing the 5–10 priorities, getting to work on them, putting the team together and making sure the business that you want to continue, serves its customers. If it doesn't it's curtains'. He's acutely aware that it's always the 'hardworking front office staff in the call centres and branches' that deliver customer service and in his role, he strives 'to talk to drivers, PAs, security people and janitors, exactly as I would talk to the Chair'.

Niall believes that people focus 'too much on leadership and not enough on followership' as ultimately you need to take and keep people on the journey. Leaders have to be tough and always have to be confident (but not arrogant) and can't seem overawed, as staff are nervous. Management 'isn't about Churchillian rhetoric or George Patton style leadership, it's about being clear on what you are trying to do, communicating clearly, showing staff you care by listening and answering their questions, making sure their issues get addressed and thanking them'. Humility and a sense of humour, sometimes at your own expense, are crucial. As crises are by definition all difficult and turnarounds take time, there are a lot of tough days, 'you need to be resilient and most of all you need to want to do it'.

'Reputation is critical and can be managed' says Niall, adding 'the Co-op Bank wouldn't have survived if it didn't have a good reputation with customers, as investors wouldn't have invested in it'. He stresses that in financial services, organisations have to have good reputations with audiences beyond customers, shareholders and staff, particularly with regulators. He says 'having a reputation for caring about customers, getting things done and telling it like it is, is absolutely critical otherwise you won't have a licence to operate. In the UK, after customers, the regulator is the next most important stakeholder − more important than shareholders'. At both Household Finance Corporation and Co-op Bank, the media interest was intense − but ultimately transitory, though Niall says, 'it's hard to see that when you are in the eye of the storm'. However, a 'drip drip drip of bad news' must be avoided, 'as it undermines everything'.

Niall believes that banks have, if anything, fared better reputationally, than they could have done, as they probably haven't been held to account enough for poor acquisitions made and for poor customer treatment.

He sees some politicians managing their reputation too aggressively, 'so it looks managed and easy to see through'. He adds that, 'in some cases reputation management is just spin and where that is easily seen through, it doesn't work and can have the opposite effect to that intended' . And while, as a Scottish Presbyterian, he would like to think reputation comes to reflect reality, 'inevitably the timing is out of sync'.

The impact of social media means that communications professionals will have to 'up their game in terms of pace and decisiveness'. He admires the way that in 2018 Australian cricket 'quickly and severely' dealt with the issue of cheating (in the form of 'ball tampering') by its players and quickly 'killed' the story. However, he regrets that sometimes social media doesn't allow people a second chance ('the tide can become an uncontrollable tsunami') and that this makes recovery more difficult. He adds that 'you also need to be able to stand up to social media bullying as we did at the Co-op Bank over some account closures'. On the flip side, he sees social media as reducing cover ups and obfuscation and making companies more accountable, sorting out their mistakes more quickly. He suspects that 'social media has made reputations more volatile and the management of reputations even more important'.

Asked about his biggest decisions, he cites two, both in his time with HSBC's Household Finance Corporation in the United States. In late 2007, he turned down a proposal to increase exposure to second mortgage lending – 'even though the other 19 people in the room were in favour' – which probably saved HSBC 'a couple of billion dollars'. Then, 18 months later, he decided to close the mortgage business and sell branches and other businesses, allowing HSBC to deploy capital in faster growing Asia, boosting returns for shareholders. Neither of these decisions were easy or popular, but as he says, to do this job you need 'some degree of political finesse and a very tough hide'.

THE OXFAM SCANDAL: THE BURSTING OF NGOs' REPUTATIONAL BUBBLE?

Hazel Westwood

Senior Teaching Fellow, University of Birmingham, UK

Supported by Dr Caroline Marchant
Lecturer, University of Edinburgh Business School, UK

The case of the Oxfam Scandal in 2018, provides new lessons for responsible and strategic management of reputation in the third sector. It highlights the dangers of NGOs relying too much on an historical 'halo effect' (Coombs and Holladay, 2006) at the expense of transparency. The scandal, the charity's cover-up, together with much of its subsequent crisis communications, provides a textbook example of how too narrow a focus on protecting reputation can result in any organisation worsening, rather than limiting damage to its brand. This case demonstrates the need for a more strategic, pro-active and responsible approach to reputation management, especially for NGOs.

THE CASE

More than 200 Oxfam staff played heroic roles in the aftermath of the 2010 Haiti Earthquake. An example of life-saving, humanitarian and ethical behaviour on which the charity's brand was built over the last 75 years. Except, it's since become widely known that seven Oxfam workers, including senior staff, were sexually exploiting Haitian women during the aid efforts. The scandal jars against the charity's vision and its pre-crisis image; once revealed it caused predictable unprecedented damage to its reputation. In one of the many uncomfortable twists of this case, the involvement of senior staff in the sex scandal exacerbated perceptions of charity as exploiter; a misuse of power over victims which drew Oxfam's very values into question.

Initially in 2011, in an attempt to limit reputational damage, the charity initially held its own internal investigation into the scandal. Although it announced that its country director in Haiti had resigned, it did not reveal the nature of the misconduct. The frame for the charity's lack of accountability and transparency was set by this fundamentally flawed response.

IGNORING ORGANISATIONAL VALUES

Oxfam CEO Mark Goldring was quoted on Sky News, saying hiding the full facts of the scandal was 'a sensible decision at the time, because the last thing we wanted was for the public to think they shouldn't be supporting Oxfam's work when it was bringing life-saving assistance to hundreds of thousands of people' (2018). It's a defence based on Teleological ethics – an approach in public relations which justifies a course of action based on the overall impact it will have on people. But in Oxfam's case that decision also conveniently protected income from public donations and the UK government – until the scandal inevitably became public in 2018 and contradicted their core values of 'empowerment, accountability and inclusiveness' (2013).

Oxfam's failure to inform the Charity Commission and the UK Government Dept. for International Development demonstrated a lack of both transparency and respect for stakeholders. Concealing details from regulators and funders leaves a strong image of Oxfam as culturally flawed, guarding its income stream and reputation above the needs of the vulnerable people they purport to protect. Workers who partook in sexual exploitation in humanitarian disaster zones have left quietly with job references to join other NGOs. The cover-up decision, driven by short-term damage limitation, created longer-term safe-guarding and accountability issues which impacts the whole charity sector.

CRISIS COMMUNICATIONS – A MIS-GUIDED APPROACH

There's little evidence Oxfam was working to any crisis communications plan when it initially knee-jerked a highly defensive response, inappropriate for this 'preventable' crisis type. The higher the level of responsibility for the crisis, the more accommodating the response should be. Yet Goldring's catalogue of defensive responses demonstrate a continued focus on defending reputation, rather than any genuine effort to correct mistakes, be accountable or initiate safe-guarding action. Hence, this was a missed opportunity to take a societal and sector lead approach to ensure better protection of vulnerable people in the future.

Damaging Responses from the CEO:

- 'What did we do? Murder babies in their cots?' (Swinford and Bird, 2018) Classed as 'attacking the accuser', a crisis response only appropriate when an organisation is falsely accused (Coombs and Holladay, 2012). Goldring was later forced to apologise for this 'inappropriate' comment in front of a UK Government Select Committee as it sought answers about the handling of the scandal.

- Goldring claimed the 'half-truths' of Oxfam's initial investigation were defensible (for the greater good of the people), seeking to justify the cover-up with the implicit self-judgement that the charity had done more good than harm in Haiti (Swinford and Bird, 2018). This response seeks to 'excuse' a lack of transparency.

As ambassadors, including Archbishop Desmond Tutu, publicly withdrew their support for the charity, its CEO was still failing to grasp the reality and level of public opinion. Media incredulity over his inappropriate responses to the scandal magnified the charity's poor crisis communications when contrasted with the more accommodating and considered answers from the eloquent Oxfam Director, Winnie Byanyima, who apologised, promising to root out exploiters within the charity.

CONCLUSION AND RECOMMENDATIONS

When businesses fail in transparency, accountability and in managing reputation it's likely to cause a fall in customer loyalty, sales and share price. But consequences for NGOs are more serious: a potential loss of trust impacts revenue, which diminishes operational capacity and that could cost lives. The Oxfam Scandal should therefore act as a wake-up call across the third sector that charities are not immune to the impacts of mismanaged reputation, and are, as noted in Oxfam's own values, 'accountable'. This is the premise of a number of recommendations for third sector organisations as they consider their blueprint for reputation management.

BLUEPRINT FOR REPUTATION MANAGEMENT BY NGOs

- Base reputation management decisions on a moral code or set of values (deontological ethics), particularly when supporting the vulnerable. Never compromise these values.

- Inform responses to crises by classifying crisis type according to likely organisational responsibility.

- Use accommodating crisis communications responses when attributions of responsibility are high.

- Use stakeholder mapping to consider all parties' communications needs. Be quick to report any crisis to stakeholders, including the media and regulators.

- Consider crisis victims first.

- Bring the lens of public and stakeholder opinion into the decision-making room.

- You cannot manage reputation if you are compromising accountability and transparency.

- Swiftly root out irresponsible behaviour, lead and communicate the future agenda for change.

FURTHER READING

For those seeking a deeper dive into the worlds of crisis management and crisis communication, I recommend Andrew Griffin's *Crisis, Issues And Reputation Management* (2014).

For some of the best writing on individual crises, I enjoyed Rupert Younger and David Waller writing on a range of organisations, particularly BP (The Reputation Game: The Art of Changing How People See You, 2017, pp. 145–53).

11

THE FORCES SHAPING
REPUTATION TODAY

Anyone who says that managing reputation today is more or less the same as it's always been, hasn't been paying attention.

The instantaneous world we now live in has changed everything. There is sometimes virtually no time to consider decisions, particularly on whether or how to communicate in a crisis. This chapter looks at eight of the forces and factors shaping reputation today.

THE SPEED OF SOCIAL MEDIA JUDGEMENT

In 2015, 72-year-old Sir Tim Hunt was a Noble Laureate and one of Britain's leading scientists. He'd worked at University College London (UCL) for almost 20 years. Speaking at a conference in Seoul he made a clumsy, inappropriate joke, when he said, 'Three things happen when [girls] are in the lab. You fall in love with them, they fall in love with you and when you criticise them, they cry' (McKie, 2015). Twitter went into meltdown. Hunt went to bed, got up and did one mediocre radio interview and caught his plane home. By the time he landed in London, his career was effectively over. He had been given little option but to resign his job. The European Science Council also asked him to stand down. His feminist wife and other people stood up for him, but it was too late. According to his wife, Professor Mary Collins, UCL 'cared only for their reputation and not about the well-being of their staff' (McKie, 2015).

Reputation Management and Social Media

Interview with Simon Lewis

Chief Executive of AFME and formerly the first Communications Secretary to The Queen and Director of Communications at No 10 Downing Street. Simon has also held senior roles with Vodafone, Centrica and NatWest. He is a visiting Professor at the Cardiff School of Journalism. Simon was appointed an OBE in the 2014 New Year Honours List for public service and services to international education through the Fulbright Commission.

Over the course of my career I have seen at first-hand how reputational management has become a crucial part of how a well-run organisation operates. The same discipline and approach works across both the private and public sectors and in organisations of different sizes. It starts from the premise that it is possible to measure and then manage an organisation's reputation and to build effective programmes to both protect and enhance reputation. It also works on the basis that a reputational crisis can and should be managed as effectively and systematically as any other crisis whether financial, physical or organisational.

The most seismic change in reputation management over the last 20 years has been the growth and impact of social media. The death of the Princess of Wales in 1997 was probably the last global news event of the pre-internet era. At that time, there were only 10 million regular users of the internet and the news agenda was dominated by the traditional media and newspapers in particular. Big news stories were broken exclusively on television or radio.

Since then, reputation management has taken public relations, an industry I joined 30 years ago, from a tactical skill to a strategic discipline which has a critical role to play at the centre of any organisation. I have seen at first hand in my roles in the corporate sector and at Buckingham Palace and Number 10 Downing Street, how effective reputation management can help shape the direction of an organisation, particularly at time of significant change. Understanding and working with, rather than against, social media is a crucial part of this process.

In the midst of the social media storm, there is sometimes only one way to survive. And that can be to act clearly and decisively — and quickly. And get the big calls right.

With the undeniable link between behaviour and reputation amplified in the digital age you can forget about being all things to all people. Just focus on those who matter, those with influence and develop a thicker skin.

Kevin Soady (Partner, Kekst CNC)

But the speed of events is only one dimension of our changed world. The sources of information and opinion have multiplied many fold. In addition, many of the players, from Governments to NGOs, are much more ambitious (or at least more interventionist) than they once were.

THE NGO, CITIZEN, JOURNALIST, CHARITY, LOBBYIST, ACTIVIST AND MASS MOVEMENT

In a complex world of information overload, people want to make sense of it. And they don't particularly trust politicians or companies to do that. This has created a huge opportunity for organisations that have a campaigning social purpose, like charities and NGOs.

NGOs have suffered reputational damage in 2017/18. In the previous chapter, Hazel Westwood of the University of Birmingham, skilfully dissected Oxfam's handling of its crisis in Haiti. However, this has not (yet) fundamentally diminished their influence. In the prevailing liberal democratic environment, in the battle between an NGO and a corporation or Government, the NGO is almost certain to win.

But it's not limited to NGOs, the trust void can also be filled by a mass of bloggers, citizen journalists and people who tell everyone what they've seen and what they believe.

And from this comes the leaderless, often spontaneous, often wonderful, mass movements like #BlackLivesMatter and #MeToo.

In this power shift, many of these players have raised their ambition from simply highlighting problems. They now want to force change too. Britain's Health and Social Care Committee called celebrity campaigner Jamie Oliver to give evidence in May 2018. He called for fundamental changes in advertising to curb the 'relentless advertising of high salt, fat, sugar products to kids' (Davies, 2018). And for the soft drinks levy to be extended to sugary milk products. For food manufacturers, these are business changing policies.

Taking this further, new kinds of organisation have emerged. One example is the International Consortium of Investigative Journalists (ICIJ), the organisation behind the Panama Papers and the Paradise Papers. It is a US not — for — profit organisation that is fully funded by donations. It is not a traditional media organisation as it does not need readers or sales to grow. It is not a traditional NGO as it uses journalistic methods and techniques. It is not a traditional charity either. Both law firms whose documents formed the basis of these Papers claim their data was hacked and stolen. The best description of the ICIJ is a policy and lobbying charity that uses investigative journalistic methods to try to change the world.

These new forces and organisations, let's call them the NGO, citizen, journalist, charity, lobbyist, activist and mass movement, have profoundly changed reputation management. They are powerful enough to bring an organisation down, without even existing. And they are almost always more trusted than a company or a Government.

This is prompting companies to ask themselves whether they should take a stand and become a 'corporate activist', a concept discussed by Matt Painter of Ipsos MORI at the end of this chapter.

HOW JOURNALISM IS RESPONDING TO CORPORATE AND GOVERNMENT POWER

Traditional media is under pressure all over the world, usually with very stretched journalistic resources. At the same time, Governments and corporations have invested heavily in communications expertise and usually have the additional advantage of planning the timing of key announcements.

But journalism is fighting back. With the Panama and Paradise Papers the ICIJ (mentioned above) built and co-ordinated a global network of journalists by partnering with 100 media organisations worldwide. These include the BBC, New York Times, Asahi Shimbun, Le Monde and ABC. By working together for over a year on each project, the journalists turned the tables. When the news became public, it was the journalists who were well organised. It was Governments and companies that were scrambling to respond.

In the demise of Cambridge Analytica, British TV station Channel 4 secretly filmed 'Bosses [...] talking about using bribes, ex-spies, fake IDs and sex workers' (2018). They would never have obtained this evidence any other way.

To prove that British retailer Sports Direct did not, effectively, pay the minimum wage, two *Guardian* journalists worked there undercover for a month (Goodley and Ashby, 2015). Once again, this was probably the only way to get this story.

We mention whistle-blowers later in this chapter. In countries such as the UK, morally motivated leaks from inside organisations probably have a bigger impact than legally defined whistle-blowers. These are another key tool in ensuring that journalism can continue to hold the powerful account.

Great countries need great journalists with the freedom to operate. I asked Dow Jones CEO Will Lewis to write for this book and his essay on the future of journalism is at the end of this chapter.

INTERVENTIONIST GOVERNMENTS AND REGULATORS

In 1849 Henry David Thoreau said, the best government is 'that which governs least' (2010), but he wouldn't find many modern politicians that agree with him. Most developed countries are in the grip of a progressive, socially liberal consensus with Governments that intervene heavily in daily life. (as the BBC's Kamal Ahmed highlights in Chapter 7, it's too early to judge whether Donald Trump is a blip on the chart or a change in direction).

Governments are going to legislate the minutiae of daily life, from the level of sugar and fat in what we eat, to the amount that can be gambled in one game. Almost every major company in the world's developed countries can benefit from government action, or be disadvantaged by it.

In May 2018, the British Government reduced from £100 to £2 the maximum stake that can be gambled per bet in gaming machines (FOBTs) in betting shops on British High Streets. This move came as a surprise, the expectation had been a maximum stake of £20. These machines are responsible for 50% of the turnover of Britain's betting shops.

Governments, particularly of strong countries, don't confine their interventions to their own borders. The Foreign Account Tax Compliance Act (FATCA) was passed by the US Government in 2010. It requires foreign financial Institutions (even if not regulated in the USA) to collect data on their clients that are US citizens and transmit it to US tax authorities. At their own expense.

Just as governments intervene more and more in daily life of citizens, the regulators they have established do the same in daily business life.

Understanding government and attempting to influence policy has therefore become an essential part of corporate life. Although I see many organisations that are still, primarily, recipients of legislation rather than participants in trying to shape the rules of the game.

The difficult issue for business, is that governments and regulators are unpredictable. They both lead the agenda and follow it. Very often, in a modern Western democracy, the best way to influence government is to influence society. And that means taking more risks, being braver and becoming a 'corporate activist'.

THE DISSATISFIED WORLD

In the Battle for Truth in Chapter 4, Richard Edelman describes a world 'unwilling to believe information'. *Ipsos Global Trends* (2017) shows the world some way short of satisfaction. Across 23 countries surveyed, the majority are overwhelmed by the choices in life, under pressure to be successful, feel the world is changing too fast and wish life was simpler.

This pervading sense that life hasn't quite met expectations, underpins the decline in trust in companies and Governments. For anyone managing reputation, it is important to be cognisant of it. It's easy to dismiss dissatisfaction as an inevitability in the modern world. How can most people in a consumerist society be happy in real life, given the images they're bombarded with and the fantasy offered by the gaming world?

It's more likely that this feeling is caused by increasing inequality. And if that's the case, companies that desire a good reputation will need to be seen to be addressing this as I discuss in greater length in Chapter 12.

QUESTIONING EMPLOYEES AND WHISTLE-BLOWERS

I watched a mini soap opera unfold in a British company in 2017. An employee on a night out, tweeted something not entirely favourable about the company they worked for. Their boss texted them saying, 'remember who you work for'. The employee then tweeted a screen grab of their boss's text.

Gone are the days when people blindly follow their CEO just because they're on the payroll. Trust and respect have to be earned with employees, just as they do with customers.

For this reason, employees have become one of the key shapers of reputation. It is not possible to be a great company with a great reputation without a great culture and an engaged workforce.

One of the best ways to ensure that everyone does the right thing when no one is watching, is for other employees to refuse to accept bad behaviour, particularly from their boss. This ability to criticise and complain, reasonably, is essential to the long-term health of any organisation.

If complaints are not acted on, employees have a difficult choice. For this reason, governments are continuing to introduce legislation protecting whistle-blowers. I still see many organisations institutionally opposed to whistle-blowers. The corporate world will be a better place, particularly in sectors like financial services or hospitals, when genuine whistle-blowers are welcomed.

CUTTING THROUGH THE WHITE NOISE

In Chapter 4, Stephen Hahn-Griffiths cited 'overcoming white noise' as part of his five-point plan to win on reputation. The drumbeat of constant publicity is valuable as part of an integrated marketing programme but often does little to build reputation.

Strategic communications programmes should now all have a short, medium and long-term dimension. The emphasis should be on the big things. Take any company you know and ask yourself what they did in the last year. At best, we remember one or two positive things per company per year. Sometimes nothing.

The answer is to deliver fewer and bigger initiatives properly (that fit with the organisation's values). In the UK, John Lewis' Christmas advertising campaign mentioned by Danny Rogers in Chapter 2, is a good example. Another is VISA's partnership with the Olympics (1986–2020). My favourite is probably the creation of Louvre Abu Dhabi, instigated in 2007, as part of a 30-year partnership between the City of Abu Dhabi and the French Government.

CORPORATE TIMIDITY

Faced with a plethora of dynamic forces shaping reputation it would be logical to think that most corporations are on the verge of becoming 'corporate activists'. But they aren't.

In Britain, Europe and the United States, corporations are gripped by a new timidity. The business sector is still behind society's expectations on so many agendas including gender pay, BAME, LGBTI, sustainability, ethics, taxation, executive remuneration and inequality. This leads to a defensive feeling in the Boardroom.

Most organisations are now forensically aware of the risks they face and have developed a highly effective crisis, play book for all situations. And in the #MeToo world, the prospect of becoming a corporate activist seems like another risk.

> *Leaders need to develop their own personal narrative. Humanising the corporate-speak should be an objective for every boardroom. It is no longer enough to be able to read nicely PR-written and legally edited texts in the correct posture, with just the right amount of a smile. Leaders need to sound like real people not just tick the body language boxes.*
>
> Kevin Soady (Partner, Kekst CNC)

Furthermore, the experience of the US Election and UK's Brexit Referendum of 2017 made senior management aware of the differences in outlook between them and many of their colleagues. This has accentuated a 'them and us' perception.

I regret the impact of all of this. Business (and often capitalism) is becoming less understood and less popular in many countries. The timidity of business is leaving the debating floor open to its detractors. This won't be reversed until more CEOs speak up and more companies take a position on the big issues.

A LANGUAGE APART

It would be easier if businesses spoke the same language as their customers. Instead, companies often use words that human beings just don't. Last year, I was asked if I could 'evaluate discoverability' and I realised that some people use those words in real life. In fact, almost the whole of the financial and investor community talks in this convoluted way.

Former *Financial Times* journalist, the great Lucy Kellaway, ran her own annual 'corporate jargon awards'. In January 2017, her winner was eBay for announcing 'we are passionate about harnessing our platform to empower millions of people by levelling the playing field for them'. She also commended Infosys for describing a redundancy programme as an 'orderly ramp down'. When she left her job in journalism to become a teacher, she concluded that 'things have gone on and on getting worse' (Morton-Clarke, 2017).

The future for corporations wanting to shape their reputation amidst all of the forces outlined in this chapter has to be built on plain, honest speaking.

This chapter is completed by the two excellent essays discussing the forces shaping reputation today.

Firstly, Matt Painter, Managing Director of the Ipsos
MORI Reputation Centre discusses the risks, and rewards, of
'corporate activism'.

And finally, Dow Jones CEO and Publisher of the *Wall Street
Journal* William Lewis argues that 'we must reinvent journalism
to reassert its position as a vital element in democracy around
the world', together with a manifesto for doing just that.

TAKING A STAND – DO THE REWARDS OF CORPORATE ACTIVISM OUTWEIGH THE RISKS?

Matt Painter

Managing Director, Ipsos MORI Reputation Centre

It's not new for businesses to have a clear social purpose –
Lever Brothers at Port Sunlight and Cadbury at Bournville
were pioneers in Victorian Britain. But today, with the 'crisis
of the elites' in full flood, activist consumers and stakeholders
are pressurising corporates to show that they're on our side,
share our values and are prepared to fight our corner.

A business is judged by what it stands for – or stands up
against – as well as what it sells. In 2016, Ipsos studied
across 23 countries, 63% of the public said they tend to buy
brands that reflect their own values (up from 54% in
2014).[22] In fast-growing economies such as India, China and
Indonesia, the proportion was higher still.

We also asked key opinion formers in the UK whether it's
right that companies should take a stand on socio-political

issues. 72% of the 82 top business journalists we surveyed and 50% of the 93 MPs said 'yes'.[23]

Members of the Ipsos Reputation Council — 130 CCOs from corporations around the world — also see a licence for their businesses to speak out. In 2017, 56% said their consumers expect them to take a stand on socio-political issues, against just 23% who disagreed. One said *"businesses are part of the community so they should have a view. Leadership should not stop at financial issues."*

One thing isn't in doubt: the decision to support or champion a cause will impact the reputation of a company. Principle may have to be weighed against pragmatism. Our research suggests some criteria for chief executives, Boards and corporate communicators as they make these decisions.

ABOVE ALL, BE RELEVANT AND AUTHENTIC

The most successful examples of corporate activism are when a business has something to say, not when it has to say something.

Not every firm can emulate American clothing company Patagonia, a self-described 'activist company' whose support of environmental causes is 'the reason we're in business' (2018). But blue-chip Qantas is an equally powerful example of progressive activism, through its support for same-sex marriage in Australia. CEO Alan Joyce explained 'Qantas has always spoken up on gender issues, on LGBTI issues, on indigenous issues and we will continue to do so and no attempt at bullying us into suppressing our voice will work (*Guardian*, 2017)'.

Authenticity is crucial: 29% of the UK consumers we surveyed[24] said that companies that speak out on social and political topics are merely opportunists. People are quick to sniff out campaigns which are self-interested, trivialising or bandwagon-jumping.

On the other hand, a stance which reflects a genuine social purpose can bring benefits beyond the purely altruistic — a connection with customers, an edge in the battle for talent and a voice in policy debates. This is doing well by doing good.

PRACTISE WHAT YOU PREACH

Any stance will lack credibility if the company can't show a track record of action. If you're being vocal about diversity, you'd better be sure you measure up within your own business. And wherever possible, show the tangible value of your work to people's lives.

As one Ipsos Reputation Council member remarked: 'It has to be relevant, it has to be in context, and there have to be actions'.

EVALUATE THE RISKS

Taking a bold stand is inherently divisive and can be a bruising experience. Activism might bring rewards, but it will definitely carry risks.

A total of 59% Ipsos Reputation Council Members believe the benefits of taking a stand are bigger than ever. But 77% say the risks are greater, too. So, it's important to be selective. Speaking out on issues which are closely aligned with party politics, such as Brexit or the Trump presidency, will be especially polarising.

FOR SOME, DISCRETION IS THE BETTER PART OF VALOUR

Really taking a stand — not just hitching your wagon to the latest trend — means dealing with opposing points of view. CEOs and CCOs have to gauge how a position will impact their corporate reputation in different parts of the world or among audiences with conflicting expectations (not least their own employees). They may have regulatory restrictions on what they can say. Good research, consultation and planning are crucial.

Businesses with less appetite for outright controversy can engage collectively, via trade associations or industry bodies. They are not, perhaps, taking a confrontational stand, but are still expressing a principled point of view and contributing to the debate.

SOCIETY NEEDS TRADITIONAL MEDIA TO SURVIVE AND FLOURISH — BUT WE NEED TO DO MORE TO PROVE IT

William Lewis

CEO, Dow Jones, and Publisher of The Wall Street Journal

Frank and fearless journalism is a key component of any properly functioning democracy. It is a truism that has been trotted out for decades — by political scientists and pundits and even politicians themselves (albeit through gritted teeth, in the case of some elected representatives). Those of us proud to have called ourselves journalists have burnished it as a badge of honour. Who wouldn't want to be the sheriff bringing the bad guys to book?

Yet, in an era of doubt, division and distrust for many in the West's more mature democracies, it is an article of faith that has been shaken by a range of forces – economic, political, cultural and of course, digital.

The last few years have been a tumultuous time for journalism – perhaps even for the whole notion of truth telling. A time when many people believe they can find a version of the news that suits their prejudices and source comfort from a set of alternative facts.

Clearly, those who set out to deliberately propagate fake news for political, commercial or vindictive reasons are the worst offenders. Almost as culpable, though, are the digital platforms that distribute such content – theirs is often a crime of wilful blindness. That they do so for commercial reasons (clothed in cant about doing no evil), makes it worse.

Then there are those who throw the term 'fake news' around like confetti to undermine perfectly legitimate journalism. This poisoning of the well of sensible discourse is often more pernicious than some of the more ludicrous fake news, tales themselves. It has spread distrust and provided a cloak of plausible deniability for all manner of crooks and crackpots.

But it is not enough for traditional media to point to their lauded and laureled mastheads. 'Trust us, we've done this for years and won plenty of Pulitzers' will not cut it.

We must do more than bleat about fake news. We must champion the value and the virtue of real news. We must reinvent journalism to reassert its position as a vital element in democracy around the world.

How?

A first step is to stop taking readers and audiences for granted. For the company I lead, Dow Jones, that means membership.

People who subscribe to *The Wall Street Journal* and other products become our members. They enjoy tangible benefits for doing so: our *WSJ+* loyalty scheme grants members unique access to brilliant events, for example.

Membership gives our readers and audience a stronger, direct connection with our journalism – reinforcing its legitimacy and importance in their hearts and minds.

The point about access and experiences is critical. We call it Live Journalism. Show as well as tell. And, crucially prove.

Live Journalism also involves transparency – and transparency is vital in fostering trust. Newsrooms rarely like having the light shone on them – but most journalism need not be cloaked in secrecy. We can – and must – protect sources and scoops but still show people how we construct our stories.

We need to show people how we make what we make. Rather like organic food, we need to be frank and fearless about our ingredients in order to be authentic.

Allied to Live Journalism and transparency is good governance. What principles underpin the business and the newsroom? What systems are in place to ensure accuracy and fairness?

What is a media outlet's policy and record on corrections? What are its rules on double sourcing of stories? Are there named, contactable journalists?

Furthermore, is there a firm demarcation between news and comment? How do you ensure the line between news and advertising is not blurred by commercial interest?

Next: data. Dow Jones is now a data-centred company. Not just data about our customers, helping us better serve their interests, but also data that helps us write deeper, richer stories – inspiring profound and enduring confidence in our journalism.

Storytelling rooted in and grown out of high quality data will be essential. The best crime and health reporting should start from a data point, for example. Data provides objective truth but also context – the building blocks of great journalism and the ultimate antidote to fake news.

Finally, people.

Increasingly for us, having the right people involves a positive and sustained approach to diversity and inclusion. At Dow Jones, we have decided that women should hold at least 40% of senior management posts in every Dow Jones department. More improvements will follow.

It is vital we better reflect shifting demographics and attitudes to develop and maintain a lasting bond of trust with our readers and their changing lives.

Membership. Live Journalism. Good governance. Data. Diversity.

These are, I believe, at least some of the key ingredients required to reinforce the credibility of responsible media brands in civil society.

It is vital that we do so because, as we say at Dow Jones, where you get the news from has never been more important.

12

REPUTATION MANAGEMENT IN FUTURE

As American writer William Gibbons said, 'the future is already here, it's just not very evenly distributed yet'. (Quote Investigator, 2017)

In managing reputation, we can see the three most important trends around us now: the first is the impact of artificial intelligence (AI), the second is the need to engage directly with our unequal world and the third is the converging of many different communications and marketing disciplines into reputation management.

ARTIFICIAL INTELLIGENCE

For now, the key part of the future that is most unevenly distributed is the use of AI. In 1950s America, some of the brands that embraced television advertising ahead of their rivals, like Band-Aid, Remington Razors and M&Ms sowed the seeds for long lasting success. Maybe it will be the same with AI.

Consumer interaction with Facebook and Google is, of course, already influenced by AI. Algorithms are not only influencing what we see, but also our decisions and behaviours. And the smartest brands are spending big to enable them to keep pace. In Japan, the humanoid robot Pepper (developed by Softbank and Alderbaran) can interact with customers and perceive human emotions (Fagella, 2018). Every single successful retail brand is uniting behavioural economics and neuroscience with data and AI, or they wouldn't still be in business.

In theory, these interactions should help reputation management as more interaction will be standardised. And customer satisfaction is one of the drivers of reputation. Although only companies offering customers whatever kind of interaction they want, including human, will have the highest satisfaction levels.

AI, Bots and Journalism

I am optimistic about AI and machine learning in the context of journalism. It clearly has the potential to eradicate the errors to which humans are prone. Obviously, the algorithms need to be written with rooting out and rejecting fake news at source in mind. Also, automating the generation of effectively commodified content could well free up human journalistic talent to work on the tougher stories — the ones the bad guys really don't want us to read or watch. A machine can write up a company results story — a human can land the scoop about that same firm's CEO embezzling funds.

William Lewis, CEO, Dow Jones,
and Publisher of *The Wall Street Journal*

In the practice of reputation management, the vital data and insight element of the process are already being revolutionised by AI. Research by the UK's Chartered Institute of

Public Relations (CIPR) estimates that 12% of 'PR skills' can now be conducted by AI and that this will rise to 38% in coming years (2018).

The biggest challenge for reputation management is the combination of AI and content creation, and the ability to disseminate limitless amounts of news (or fake news). The 2017 US Election gave us a glimpse of this in action. A 2017 study by the Oxford Internet Institute found that Wikipedia pages are constantly edited and re-edited by clashing chatbots (software programmes developed to 'correct errors'). Some pages were edited and re-edited over 2,000 times a year, as far back as 2010 (Sample, 2017).

To some extent, we've been here before. In the relatively early days of the internet, some brands created seemingly independent websites to endorse themselves, until Google brought the practice to a halt.

The likeliest scenario is that some brands will unite AI, content creation and distribution ability and steal a march on others, at least for a couple of years. Some will over-reach ethical boundaries and suffer reputational damage as a result. And in the end, the rest will catch up. But the reputation manager of the future (and may be today) will lead a team with strong AI and data capabilities.

ENGAGING WITH AN UNEQUAL WORLD

We briefly discussed the dissatisfied world in Chapter 11. One of the key foundations of dissatisfaction is rising inequality over the last 20 years.

The richest 9% of the world's population own over 85% of the world's wealth. In America, the richest now own the same proportion of the nation's wealth as in the 1920s. Researchers also find links between physical and mental health[25]. If Thomas Piketty and others are right, this inequality is set to increase.

Increasing inequality is a factor in many of the surprise election results of the period 2016−2018. It also poses questions for companies and their reputation managers.

Looking to the future, it seems that in the United States and Europe, only a politician that can appeal to the mass of the electorate in an age of populism, can win. The same must therefore be true for major companies seeking a great reputation. Only a company that engages with its own community, and meets society's expectations, can maintain a great reputation.

The following sidebar suggests how the agenda might look for a company that accepts it needs to engage with an unequal world.

Agenda for Engaging with an Unequal Society

(1) *Is the Board close enough to society? Should it spend a greater proportion of the year where stakeholders are (employees, customers, intermediaries, influencers, shareholders, government and regulators) − and meet as many them as possible. Should Board meetings move around the country?*

(2) *Consider our executive pay from society's point of view: Is the level of guaranteed earnings or the rate of increase (relative to the workforce generally) unfair?*

(3) *Should we introduce a greater level of transparency than all the rules and regulations require, whether that is earnings data, environmental data or even whether senior management pay tax in the country?*

(4) *Is community engagement central to our corporate purpose (or is it isolated as 'just CSR')? Should we*

review all CSR budgets and ask whether our corporate spending reduces inequality in society? Is our spending directed to the areas of most concern to our stakeholders?

(5) Should we review recruitment policies – do they act to help the whole of society – and is it possible to meet the corporate purpose and help reduce inequality in society? Should we take and train school leavers wherever possible?

(6) Should we act ahead of any government review and ensure all stakeholders are represented at Board level (particularly employees)?

(7) Should we commit to reflecting society (or our stakeholders) at all management levels, not just in terms of gender and ethnicity, but also disability and possibly even non-university and state education backgrounds?

(8) Should we talk publicly and be higher profile in society, particularly our CEO and senior management? Should we talk more about broader issues as well as the company's products and services?

(9) Is it time to commit to reporting in more detail on more than just financials, including our impact on society and on the environment? Should we fully embrace ESG (Environmental Social Governance) reporting?

THE RISE OF 'REPUTATION MANAGEMENT'

The final of my three trends affecting the future of reputation management is the rise of the concept itself. The importance of reputation has spawned the development of reputation management as a profession. In future, the rise of reputation management as a profession will impact the management of reputation.

A LinkedIn search for 'reputation management' in June 2018 yielded nearly one million results for people citing reputation management compared to 4.3 million citing corporate communications and 10.9 million for public relations. I expect these numbers to almost reverse over the coming years.

Leading consultancies have already begun to change. The world's leading corporate consultancy, Brunswick, describes itself as 'advising on business-critical issues' (2018). By contrast, the world's largest consultancy, Edelman, partners with clients to 'promote and protect their brands and reputation' (2018). New big kid on the block, Teneo Blue Rubicon, describes its mission as 'creating value by building and protecting reputation' (2018).

This shift in consultancy positioning will impact leading organisations. The intriguing question is how will a profession that has traditionally specialised in one piece of the jigsaw respond when someone asks for the whole jigsaw?

The rest of this chapter consists of five essays from some of the leading thinkers in reputation across the Atlantic.

Paul Holmes, Founder of The Holmes Report, tackles the fascinating subject of how decisions are taken throughout an organisation. He outlines a four-point plan for the twenty-first-century reputation advisor, who needs to be more assertive, wise and courageous.

Author of *Trust Me, PR Is Dead* (2015), Robert Phillips, advocates the concept of public leadership as the replacement for public relations.

Basil Towers, Senior Managing Director, Teneo Blue Rubicon argues that reputation management has a healthy future, but only if it grows up. The key words for reputation management and for Corporate Affairs or Corporate Communications in the future are business, impact and value.

To Lewis Founder, Chris Lewis, the future is invisible in his tour de force on our social media age.

To finish the chapter, Steve Earl and Stephen Waddington, co-authors of *Brand vandals: Reputation Wreckers and How to Build Better Defences* look back on the battle between brands and vandals since their book of 2013.

THE FUTURE OF REPUTATION MANAGEMENT CONSULTANCY

Paul Holmes

Founder and Chair, The Holmes Group

The ability to manage corporate reputation – to build relationships with a company's key stakeholders, to nurture and protect those relationships and to leverage them for mutual benefit – has never been more critical.

The digital and social media age has given employees, consumers, shareholders and citizens at large access to more information (and misinformation) about corporate practices and policies than ever before. And with a significant body of research suggesting that people trust the word of friends and family more than traditionally authoritative sources, those who take a stand for or against an organisation can have a major influence on its ability to recruit talent, sell products, advance its legislative agenda or gain community support.

I have argued that in this environment, every decision an organisation makes has four broad – and equally important – implications. The first three are well understood, and formally incorporated into the decision-making process at most companies: financial implications, operational implications and legal implications. The fourth − reputational implications − is all too often an afterthought. How many organisations have a chief reputation officer with the same stature as the COO, the CFO or the chief legal counsel?

The fact that this position does not exist (yet) in even the best managed corporations is not necessarily the fault of those who occupy the C-suite or sit on the board of directors. It is, to a large extent, the fault of corporate communications, public affairs and others who have allowed their role to be defined too narrowly. The twenty-first-century reputation advisor will need to approach his or her responsibility more assertively, more wisely and more courageously.

First and foremost, reputation consultants need to ensure that they are involved in making decisions, not just communicating them. An organisation typically enjoys (or otherwise) the reputation its behaviour merits. That means if a decision − about environmental standards, employee layoffs, customer service − has the potential to impact reputation (and nearly all decisions do), the reputation consultant needs to be involved in the decision-making process.

He or she should also have access not only to the CEO, but also to the board of directors. At companies in crisis, board directors are increasingly vulnerable and may face personal liability for lapses. The chief reputation officer should have a direct line to the board. When possible, boards should include at least one member whose background includes responsibility for an organisation's reputation.

Second, reputation counsellors need to focus on corporate values. Most organisations today claim to be guided by values that go beyond the basics of making a good product and selling it at a fair price. Few live those values in a consistent way; many of the biggest crises of recent years came about because companies (Volkswagen, United Airlines, Wells Fargo and Facebook) failed to live up to their values.

The reputation counsellor should regularly ask an organisation's employees three questions: Do you know what this organisation's values are? Do you believe senior management lives up to these values? And do you personally feel empowered to incorporate these values into the way you do your job? If employees answer no to any of these questions, a crisis is likely just around the corner.

Third, the reputation counsellor needs to have not only an understanding of stakeholders' concerns about an organisation, but also an empathy for those concerns. He or she needs to be an advocate within the organisation for individuals who are impacted, sometimes adversely, by its operations. He or she should be immersed in the communities – online and off – where those people gather, and be prepared to communicate their criticisms, however unpopular or unfair, to senior management.

And fourth, the reputation counsellor needs to be proactive. In the past, this role has been largely reactive, responding to external crises or internal agendas. Today, he or she needs to be able to anticipate the issues on which an organisation may be asked to take a position. The past 12 months, particularly in the US, have shown that neutrality on significant social issues – from LGBTQ rights to the #MeToo movement, from immigration to the proliferation of guns in America – is no longer an option. Companies that fail to take a position are now perceived as favouring the status quo, and are as vulnerable to boycotts and other citizen action as companies that do take a stand. (Again, it is wise for organisations to be guided by their values).

It is time for organisations to re-evaluate the importance of managing reputation effectively.

PUBLIC RELATIONS NO MORE

Robert Phillips

Co-founder of Jericho Chambers and Author

'If you want to be more trusted as a leader', observed *The Guardian* commentator Stefan Stern, 'don't do bad things' (2017).

Five years ago, researching *Trust Me, PR Is Dead*, I came across a FTSE 100 CEO who opened every Board meeting by asking the same question: 'Right - who do we f*ck today?'. Their organisation was doing bad things.

The 'who do we f*ck today?' approach is as unsustainable as it is ugly. Corporate history — Enron, RBS, Volkswagen, Facebook, Cambridge Analytica please stand up — is littered with tearful endings. Stern thus offers a brilliant distillation of the current condition. 'Reputation' is not something to be 'managed', still less by a third-party agency. It is deeply behavioural. Good leaders don't f*ck their employees, customers or communities. No-one should need a public relations specialist to tell them this and not to do dumb things (although the PR industry has flourished by convincing leaders otherwise). Let's call this the ruthless application of common sense.

This supports my thesis that the world needs more public leadership, not more public relations. Rather than employing someone to create a mask or to ensure that the mask never slips (which of course it always does), it is better to require no mask at all. Public leadership repudiates spin, even when only gently applied. It demands courage — to do what is right and not just what is conventional, convenient or compliant. It is accountable to Public Value and uses the Common Good as its lodestar: behaving ethically, with wisdom, tolerance and justice. Actions, not words.

In this post-ethical age of networks and data, peddlers of fakery, polarised and polemic media and instant exposure, poor judgement and poor leadership are of course quickly and ruthlessly exposed. No amount of reputation or message 'management' will ever save it/you/them.

Many mischievously interpreted my 2015 book as an assault on the practice of public relations. It was not. Instead, it observed the rapidly diminishing powers of an industry which, like so many other tiring institutions of the mid- to late-twentieth century, were losing relevance while still trying to maintain status and revenues. The PR industry would, I suggested, prosper financially for some time yet — as the saying goes where there's a buyer, there's a market — but this was not to argue that it couldn't identify and arrest its own decline.

The shift from public relations to public leadership would be a positive and much-needed signal of change. Instead, we have seen countless justifications and weak arguments for evolution, not radical transformation: a kind of status quo *plus*. PR industry leaders have been fiddling while their Rome's burned.

Much of what I theorised then we now know to be true — from the rise of nasty populism, filling the vacuum of ethical public leadership, to the thirst for collaborative working and the resolution of major policy issues through new, peer-to-peer coalitions. Trusted relationships can no longer be imposed from above, if ever they could. Instead, they are shared horizontally, across networks. Effective public leadership recognises and welcomes this.

Public Leaders thus create operating frameworks based on new principles – understanding the world as it is, not as it once was. Their leadership is open, adaptive and collaborative; activist in spirit and approach. They are prepared to embrace the messy chaos and not default to platitudes and soundbites. They welcome dissent, accepting that it's OK to not have all the answers and to sometimes say they just don't know. They demonstrate genuine vulnerability, even to their implacable opponents, to build greater trustworthiness across stakeholders and communities. In the shift from public relations to public leadership, just as these new principles are required, so is a new generation of leaders to embed them. This runs to the heart of the important debate on equality and inclusion, race and age, as well as gender.

The public leadership model works. Over the past four years, together with my Jericho colleagues, we have been effecting change for a better society – working with major companies and organisations to build coalitions and consensus, based on new operating principles, and rooted in the common good. Better policy is emerging: on responsible tax, the future of work, the digital economy, transport and the built environment. Together, we can build a stronger economy and a better democracy – but only if we are prepared to address major societal issues head-on. None of us should shy away from our responsibilities to fellow citizens and society, even if it means going against the mainstream flow or putting people and planet before profit. Human value trumps shareholder value, every time. This is public leadership made real.

Nobody said the shift would be easy. Bravery is absolutely required. But wallowing in the failed practices and nostalgia of the last century and its diminished institutions is certainly not the answer to today's challenges of leadership and trust.

Those working at the vanguard of corporate change understand this to be true. There is little point hiding behind an army of lawyers or PR people — seeking false comfort in artificially created happy endings, which will eventually erode and fail. Old PR belongs in a world of make-believe. Now is the time for radical honesty, radical transparency, real action and courage. All are needed if we are to recover from the current malignant condition.

In this interregnum, meanwhile, everything can start with a single, simple step. Stop doing bad things. Don't f*ck anyone now. It's not complicated.

THE FUTURE OF REPUTATION MANAGEMENT

Basil Towers

Senior Managing Director, Teneo Blue Rubicon

Reputation management has a healthy future. But only if it grows up.

As practitioners, we face two defining questions: can we make trust and reputation management a truly effective determinant of strategic, operational or commercial success for businesses and organisations? And what will it take to get there?

To answer that, fast forward five years. Businesses that have risen to this challenge will have certain characteristics quite different to those we commonly see today.

A SHORT AND LONG-TERM VALUE APPROACH

Most fundamentally, the leaders and boards of those businesses will have an absolute focus on the reputations and the trust which the business needs to win.

They will have moved far beyond lazy legacy thinking and generic, one-size-fits models, and will see their multiple reputations for what they are: complex and dynamic assets of value.

Leaders will understand that the impact of these intangibles may not be immediate or indeed visible. That reputation and trust can erode slowly and threaten the sustainability of the business model or to future cash flows as well as having an immediate impact on revenues, margins and the P & L.

Leaders will watch constantly for signs of corrosion, using effective measurement tools to provide an early warning.

Crucially, they will accept their accountability for trust and reputation, and expect to be held to account by their boards as well as stakeholders.

A STRATEGIC APPROACH

And from that focus and that accountability, other characteristics of success will follow — for senior leaders, for the specialists focusing on helping the business manage reputation and for everyone across the business.

The active trust and reputation building strategies they draw up will include, on the one hand, the outcomes of business choices, actions and culture, and, on the other hand, the impacts of engagement, relationships and communications — what the business does, how it does it and what it says.

Strategies will strike an effective balance between enabling the business to compete and win while also anticipating and managing the risks that can lead to losing. The indicators used to measure the strategy's success or failure will be clearly aligned with business KPIs.

Leaders will expect the reputation strategy to help deliver the corporate strategy and annual business plans, and will expect to see it embedded within these plans and day-to-day decision-making.

AN ORGANISATIONAL CAPABILITY

Leaders will also recognise reputation management as an essential organisational capability – something the business must be good at to succeed.

Managers everywhere will be expected to have a clear understanding of the way multiple reputations and levels of trust drive business performance – in the short, medium and long-term. Every employee will be expected to understand their contribution and take responsibility.

They will be empowered and incentivised to build reputation into day-to-day operational decision making across the value chain and will be held accountable.

A sensitivity to reputation – the ability to manage the business with trust or reputation as an outcome – will be more highly valued and will be an explicit capability.

Boards and ExCos will consider the need for a reputation risk appetite statement. Reputation risk will be given more time and space for debate. It will be treated as both a risk category and the consequence of other risks materialising. Management processes and capabilities will be subject to oversight, scrutiny and compliance.

For managers, reputation risk will be part of end-to-end decision-making and planning. Often it will be critical to passing through a stage gate.

HIGHER VALUE FUNCTIONS

Finally, what of the experts most directly charged with helping the business build the trust and manage the reputations of most value?

Whether they are a broader Corporate Affairs team or a narrower Communications function they will be guided by a clear purpose — helping create and protect value in the business.

The team will influence what the business *does*, as well as what it *says* — early. It will provide reputational intelligence and insights to help the business make better decisions, and to assess and plan for their consequences.

Its leaders will operate as advisers and behave as enablers. They will speak the language of the business. And as today, the function will provide the narrative and campaigns and support the moments that build trust.

These teams will be lean, agile and collaborative, moving resource to where it can have the greatest impact.

The key words for reputation management and for Corporate Affairs or Communications in the future are business, impact and value.

THE FUTURE IS INVISIBLE

Chris Lewis

Founder and CEO, LEWIS

Transparency. Everyone's talking about it. Social and digital media enable an army of amateur commentators. They're everywhere at all times. They are ready to report wrongdoing wherever they see it. If you're a celebrity, they're watching you when you do ordinary things and lip-reading every muttered indiscretion. Our industry tells high-profile individuals and corporations to be on their guard against this new age of constant scrutiny. This should drive a new golden age of responsible behaviour. But it hasn't. Social media has been with us for over a decade and if anything, the level of wrong-doing has increased. Let's review the facts.

Our leaders have illegally avoided taxes, lied about emissions in the car industry, rigged interest rates, sheltered customers from taxes, laundered Mexican drug money, presided over an offshore banking system that was larger than anyone ever thought, forced good companies into closure and destroyed pension funds as they themselves grew wealthier. They oversaw unprecedented destruction of wealth and the collapse of the financial system and watched as life savings placed into investment funds set up by leaders of unimpeachable integrity turned out to be Ponzi schemes. Our spiritual leaders have covered up sex abuse in the Church. Our charity leaders have sexually abused the vulnerable. Our child welfare leaders have permitted child abuse.

Our political leaders have allowed an epidemic of gun crime. They have cheated on their expenses and admitted sexually inappropriate behaviour. Education leaders have presided over exam cheating and sexual harassment. Our defence industry leaders have settled claims relating to the bribery of government officials. Our leaders of public utilities have poisoned customers. Our entertainment leaders are facing multiple allegations of sexual harassment and abuse. Our leading broadcasters have falsely accused political figures of being child abusers, while allowing actual abusers to commit crimes on their premises. Meanwhile, our sporting leaders have been caught cheating and doping. Our medical leaders have chronically mistreated patients. Our human rights lawyers have been struck off for misconduct and dishonesty while our military leaders have admitted using torture and our service personnel have died through their negligence.

You might argue that social media at least allows us to know this. It hasn't though slowed or stopped it happening.

If anything, it's the opposite. But why? Well, sometimes because the story just ain't true. We've seen multiple cases of fake news. This is because frankly, people prefer entertainment to education. The latter involves too much work and nuance.

It remains easy though to hide an unpleasant truth because the very thing that makes social media so powerful is what makes it weak.

It can be hidden in the sheer volume of noise. It can be hidden in amnesia. There is so much overload that most of us can barely remember what happened this morning, let alone yesterday. It can be hidden in ambiguity and lazy half-truths. Beliefs are more important than facts. Sir Bradley Wiggins is most certainly and factually not a drug cheat. But what do you think? British politicians are not any more corrupt than before, but what do you think? The world is a much better place by any medical, economic or social measure, but really, what do you think?

It can be hidden in tokenism. Carefully placed images of superficial representation can easily hide an unchanged reality.

It can be hidden in images and presentation. A CEO or politician can be trained to make eye contact with a camera. Or to answer a question with a question. Does this make them actually more truthful? No. It makes them appear more truthful though.

It can be hidden in complexity-driven laziness. The genius of any public inquiry is not that it seeks to hide uncomfortable truths, but that it exposes them in such detail that no-one can be bothered. It can be hidden in text. Digital means global and that means images rather than text. Communicators know that the world consumes images faster and more universally. The corollary is also true. If you want to hide truth, then text will do just fine.

Social media itself is a manipulation of reputation suggesting the purveyor is more immediate, more modern, more receptive and, yes, more transparent.

Greater scrutiny will change the future of reputation management. This will not change the way companies and individuals act, however. It will change the way they *appear* to act at a superficial level. In this respect then, the future of reputation management will remain the same as its past. Invisibility, after all, is just another type of transparency.

WHO'LL WIN IN THE TWENTY-FIRST CENTURY: THE CORPORATIONS OR THE BRAND VANDALS?

Steve Earl
Managing Director, Europe, Zeno Group

Stephen Waddington
Partner and Chief Engagement Officer, Ketchum

Five years on from the publication of their book #BrandVandals, its authors reflect on the progress made by organisations in getting to grips with the fragmentation of media.

When it comes to reputation, there will always be winners and losers. But when it comes to reputational vandalism, you should question whether anyone ever really wins, or whether the best that can be attained is a pyrrhic victory.

The war on brands has moved on since we wrote #BrandVandals back in 2013, and #BrandAnarchy before it. Increasingly, attacks on brand reputation by activists follow something bad that the company has done, or an aspect of doing business that needs to change on moral, political or environmental grounds.

With the brand in a mess of its own making, individuals and organisations then step in to fan the flames that are already alight, rather than stirring the pot in the first place.

Yet the threat from deliberate reputational saboteurs, whether that be from aggrieved individuals or a chorus of dissenting voices, remains ever-present.

YANKING AT THE ONLINE MOB

The omnipresence of the internet, and of smartphone use for recording and sharing so many aspects of our daily lives, means that it has never been easier to capture and share wrongdoing, make a prominent point or wreak havoc through direct action and pull on the power chord of the online crowd.

So, if the weaponry is in the hands of the vandals and mobilising the mob is easier than ever, surely, they stand to win, rather than the corporations needing to change their behaviour and create more effective reputational defences?

Or is there more to gained by the brand owners who have been compelled to do better in protecting themselves, and have learned how to deal with attacks better, with that experience even enabling them to earn some reputational kudos for their actions?

Well, it can cut both ways. Brands that become activists themselves, taking a stand on prevalent issues and behaving in more human ways to give greater backbone to their existence in business stand, in theory, less chance of suffering severe reputational wounds at the hands of vandals.

But the brands' behaviour change, appetite for engagement and willingness to step forward may have been spurred by vandalism or some level of activism that targeted the brand in the first place. In which case surely the ultimate winners would be those who hit out against the brands?

BRAVERY IS IN THE EYE OF THE BEHOLDER – AND THE INTERNET

In our view it's a matter of courage. Bravery has become a corporate attribute in the intervening years since we wrote #BrandVandals.

Courageous organisations are those that are prepared to listen to their publics and stand up for what they believe in, and crucially what they don't. They're also prepared to 'fess up' to their weaknesses.

Fast food outlet KFC apologised to the UK public when its food wasn't very fast because of a shortage of supplies. Many CEOs have taken a stand and supported the actions of their brands in tackling gender diversity head-on, such as Gap's Women and Opportunity programme to nurture female leaders.

Tesla's Elon Musk quit US President Trump's Manufacturing Council over the administration's withdrawal from the Paris climate change agreement, and a swathe of business leaders followed over Trump's handling of white supremacist protests. The council was soon disbanded.

Here's the issue. A brand value only has true value if you are prepared to defend it. Organisations under increased scrutiny from their audiences are prepared to respond, and where necessary take a stand and share their genuine point of view.

As methods for assessing tangible reputational value become more established and are applied more consistently, being able to determine winners, losers and the costs of victory is becoming easier.

Our bet though is that brands will become more adept at managing unprovoked attacks, so while vandals will still manage to cause damage, the instances will become less frequent because brands will have done more to change their behaviour and determine how they apply themselves in a changing world.

Meaning that, effectively, they both win. Vandals make their point, brands evolve. Mind you, there will always be some that just get it completely wrong or make daft decisions.

Make sure that your organisation isn't one that falls foul.

Organisations begin listening — brands are starting to listen because they have no other option

Brands as activists — organisations that are prepared to stand up for their values benefit from a reputational shield, of sorts

Vandals to advocates — organisations that engage with online criticism can very quickly build advocates

Manifesto tackling #BrandVandals

13

POSTSCRIPT: REPUTATION MANAGEMENT, A FORCE FOR GOOD?

I was discussing future holiday destinations with a good friend, who's also a journalist. He said, 'they shoot people over there for telling the truth, so you'll be fine'.

This image of PR people as 'paid to lie' has been present throughout my career. And now – if the Edelman Trust Monitor is to be trusted – the public thinks the same of other professions, including politicians and, dare I say it, journalists.

In this book, I've presented reputation management as the future of public relations and corporate communications. Those activities will always exist, but as part of something much bigger. And better.

Reputation is about authenticity, behaviour, performance and communication. It's so valuable that companies, Governments and celebrities want a good reputation. And the only way to have a great reputation is to be great, but also to care about how others see you.

Everyone manages their reputation by the things they do and the decisions they take. Some manage it well, some badly. Some are managing their reputation consciously, others subconsciously. But everyone is doing it.

And those great organisations that do great things and truly care about how others see them, will manage their reputation consciously. And that is good for society. Or at least for those societies with transparent laws and regulations and a free media.

That's because these societies' expectations rise all the time. Organisations that want to keep their good reputation will have to continually improve their behaviour, at least as fast as their society expects them to.

By continually improving behaviour, great organisations will improve society. And one of the reasons they'll do it, is because they want a better reputation.

ENDNOTES

1. Find out more from the Reputation Institute in Chapter 4 on p. 51.

2. The 4th edition of the best reputation management book on the market. *Reputation Management: The Key to Corporate Communications and Public Relations* by John Doorley and Helio Fred Garcia is due to be published in 2019.

3. Waitrose prices are based on products listings on its website as of 29 May 2018 and Aldi prices are based on listings on the MySupermarket website as of 29 May 2018. Further details are found in the bibliography.

4. Small and Mid-Cap Index, Quoted Companies Alliance and BDO, Autumn 2015.

5. Demographic splits: 48% male, 52% female; company size by number of employees: Micro (1–9): 20%, Small (10–49): 15%, Medium (50–249): 19%, large (250 +): 46%; regional splits: North East: 4%, North West: 12%, Yorkshire & Humberside: 8%, East Midlands: 7%, West Midlands: 8%, East of England: 9%, London: 13%, South East: 16%, South West: 9%, Wales: 5%, Scotland: 7%, NI: 2%.

6. https://fullfact.org/economy/UK_gender_pay_gap/ cited 11.05.2018

7. The methodology includes the General Online Population, Informed Public and Mass Population. The General Online Population make up 1,150 respondents per market, reviewing seven years across 25 + markets of those aged 18 +. The Informed Public reviews 10 years in 20 + markets representing 15% of the total population – the survey includes 500 respondents in the US and China and 200 in other markets. These people must meet four criteria: ages 25–64, college educated, in top 25% of household income per age group in each market and who report significant media consumption and engagement in business news and public policy. Finally, the Mass Population includes all respondents not including Informed Public representing 85% of the total global population (methodology taken from the 2018 Executive Summary of the Edelman Trust Barometer 2018).

8. Global RepTrak® 100: Based on a methodology that measures the perceptions of the *Informed General Public*, who are somewhat or very familiar with which the companies they are being asked to evaluate, the Global RepTrak 100 represents the largest normative database on corporate reputation in the world. The study focuses on the key global economies – essentially the G15 – and provides an aggregated global and highly representative measure of reputation based on more than 230,000 individual ratings of multi-national companies. The capture of Global RepTrak data is based on a scientific online survey that is fielded in Q1 of every year. The study sets out to answer questions that every C-Suite Executive around the world should know:

   • What is my company's reputation – and how does it compare?

- How can I improve and protect my company's reputation?

- What is the business impact and ROI in better managing my company's reputation?

9. Country RepTrak® 100: Based on a methodology that measures the perceptions of the *Informed General Public* who are somewhat or very familiar with the nation they are being asked to evaluate. Primarily, Country RepTrak is based on the perceptions of the citizens who reside among the G8 industrialised nations. The study measurement focuses on the largest and most economically important countries in the world – encompassing 55 countries in total – and it provides an aggregated global measure of reputation based on more than 58,000 individual ratings aggregated across all the nations studied. This is the seventh year that study has been fielded – Country RepTrak first ran in 2011. The capturing of the Country RepTrak data is based on a scientific online survey that is fielded in Q1 of every year.

10. *The Reputation Game: The Art of Changing How People See You*, by David Waller and Rupert Younger, was published by Oneworld Publications in October 2017, price £18.99.

11. Richard H McLaren, 'Corruption: Its Impact on Fair Play', 19 Marquette Sports Law Review 15, 2008-2009, 15.

12. Jacques Rogge, President of the International Olympic Committee, 1 March 2011, reported in: Boniface, Pascal and Lacarriere, Sarah and Verschuuren, Pim and Tuaillon, Alexandre and Forrest, David and Icard, Jean-Michel and Meyer, Jean-Pierre and Wang, Xuchong,

Sports Betting and Corruption: How to Preserve the Integrity of Sport, Institute of Int. & Strategic Relations (2011), p. 4.

13. Kamal Ahmed's first book *The Life and Times of a Very British Man* published by Bloomsbury Publishing in October 2018.

14. GiveOut is a charity raising funds for lesbian, gay, bisexual, trans, queer and intersex (LGBTQI) causes worldwide. The charity enables individual donors to give through a single platform to support the global LGBTQI movement, funding activists and their organisations around the world to promote and protect the rights of LGBTQI people.

15. Read more on the ICIJ in Chapter 11.

16. The Leveson inquiry was a judicial public inquiry into the culture, practices and ethics of the British press, chaired by Lord Justice Leveson. The Inquiry published the Leveson Report in November 2012, which made recommendations for a new, statutory body to oversee a new, independent regulator to replace the existing Press Complaints Commission.

17. GFK Adimark, April 2015.

18. CADEM, April 2018.

19. Thalidomide was used in the late 1950s and early 1960s to combat morning sickness, but led to children being born without limbs. In 2012, the inventor of thalidomide, the Grünenthal Group, released a statement saying it regrets the consequences of the drug (Press Association, 2012).

20. Discover more from Niall Booker in his interview on p. 191 in Chapter 10.

21. From an exchange, 30 May 2018 with Steven Fink, Author of *Crisis Management: Planning for the Inevitable* and *Crisis Communications: The Definitive Guide to Managing the Message.*

22. Taken from the IPSOS Global Trends Survey. Base: 18,180 adults across 23 countries online survey, 12 September to 11 October 2016.

23. Taken from the IPSOS MORI Survey of UK Business & Financial Journalists (base 82) and UK member of Parliament (base 93). Face to face interview, June to August 2017.

24. 1,001 GB adults. Online. September 2017.

25. Conclusion deriding from sources at Inequality.org, accessed on 9 June 2018: https://inequality.org/

BIBLIOGRAPHY

Ahmed, K. (2008). After Obama, I can be proud of what I really am, black and white. *The Guardian*. Retrieved from https://www.theguardian.com/commentisfree/2008/nov/09/mixed-race-barackobama-lewishamilton-human-rights (Accessed on 28 May 2018).

Ahmed, K. (2008). *The life and times of a very British man.* London: Bloomsbury Publisher.

Auden, W. H., & Kronenberger, L.(Eds.) (1981). *The Viking book of aphorisms.* Dorset: Dorset Press.

BBC News. (2011). Jimmy Savile: Tributes flood in. BBC. Retrieved from http://www.bbc.co.uk/news/mobile/uk-15507826 (Accessed on 12 June 2018).

BBC News. (2011). Sir Jimmy Savile's funeral takes place at Leeds Cathedral. BBC. Retrieved from https://www.bbc.co.uk/news/uk-england-leeds-15647363 (Accessed on 12 June 2018).

Bloomberg. (2004). Online extra: Jess Bezos on word-of-mouth power. Retrieved from https://www.bloomberg.com/news/articles/2004-08-01/online-extra-jeff-bezos-on-word-of-mouth-power (Accessed on 7 May 2018).

Boniface, P., Lacarriere, S., Verschuuren, P., Tuaillon, A., Forrest, D., Icard, J.-M., ... Wang, X. (2011). Sports betting and corruption: how to preserve the integrity of sport. *Institute of International and Strategic Relations*, 4.

Brown, J. (2013). Jimmy Savile: A report that reveals 54 years of abuse by the man who groomed the nation. *The Guardian*. Retrieved from https://www.independent.co.uk/news/uk/crime/jimmy-savile-a-report-that-reveals-54-years-of-abuse-by-the-man-who-groomed-the-nation-8447146.html (Accessed on 12 June 2018).

Brunswick. (2018). *About us*. Brunswick. Retrieved from https://www.brunswickgroup.com/about-us/ (Accessed on 9 June 2018).

Channel 4 News. (2018). Cambridge analytica uncovered: Secret filming reveals election tricks. *Channel 4*. Retrieved from https://www.youtube.com/watch?v=mpbeOCKZFfQ (Accessed on 7 June 2018). Valin, Jean. Humans still needed: An analysis of skills and tools in public relations. CIPR AI panel, 2018. Retrieved from https://newsroom.cipr.co.uk/humans-still-needed—research-project-reveals-impact-of-artificial-intelligence-on-public-relations/ (Accessed on 9 June 2018).

Coombs, W. T., & Holladay, S. J. (2006). Unpacking the halo effect: Reputation and crisis management. *Journal of Communication Management*, *10*(2), 123–137. (Accessed on 2 May 2018) (doi:10.1108/13632540610664698).

Coombs, W. T., & Holladay, S. J. (2012). Parameters for crisis communication. In *The handbook of crisis communication* (pp. 17–47). Chichester: Wiley-Blackwell.

Cox, T. (2016) *4 Warren Buffet quotes about building and destroying a reputation*. Yahoo Finance. Retrieved from https://finance.yahoo.com/news/4-warren-buffett-quotes-building-105136800.html?guccounter=1 (Accessed on 29 May 2018).

Davies, C. (2018). Jamie Oliver urges MPs to tackle 'catastrophe' of childhood obesity. *The Guardian*. Retrieved from https://www.theguardian.com/lifeandstyle/2018/may/01/jamie-oliver-mps-tackle-catastrophe-childhood-obesity (Accessed on 11 June 2018).

Deloitte. (2017). The Deloitte global centre for corporate governance. Women in the boardroom: A global perspective. Retrieved from https://www2.deloitte.com/content/dam/Deloitte/za/Documents/technology-media-telecommunications/za_Wome_in_the_boardroom_a_global_perspective_fifth_edition.pdf (Accessed on 1 June 2018).

Donnan, S., & Fleming, S. (2015). Christine Lagarde calls for shake-up of bankers' pay, *The Financial Times*. Retrieved from https://www.ft.com/content/83e68f42-f407-11e4-bd16—00144feab7de (Accessed on 30 May 2018).

Doorley, J., & Garcia, H. F. (2011). *Reputation management: The key to corporate communications and public relations* (pp. 11–14). New York: Routledge.

Durando, J. BP's Tony Hayward: 'I'd like my life back'. *USA Today*, 2010. Retrieved from http://content.usatoday.com/communities/greenhouse/post/2010/06/bp-tony-hayward-apology/1#.Wx-PTyAh270 (Accessed on 5 June 2018).

Earl, S., & Waddington, S. (2013). *Brand vandals: Reputation wreckers and how to build better defences.* London: Bloomsbury Publishing.

Eccles, N., & Shatz. (2007). Reputation and its risks. *Harvard Business Review*. Retrieved from https://hbr.org/2007/02/reputation-and-its-risks (Accessed on 29 May 2018).

Edelman.(2018). *2018 Edelman trust barometer reveals record-breaking drop in trust in the U.S.* Edelman Retrieved from https://www.edelman.com/news-awards/2018-edelman-trust-barometer-reveals-record-breaking-drop-trust-in-the-us (Accessed on 12 June 2018).

Edelman.(2018). *2018 executive summary*. Edelman. Retrieved from http://cms.edelman.com/sites/default/files/2018-02/2018_Edelman_TrustBarometer_Executive_Summary_Jan.pdf (Accessed on 13 June 2018).

Edelman.(2018). *Who are we?* Edelman. Retrieved from https://www.edelman.co.uk/about/ (Accessed on 9 June 2018).

Fagella, D. (2018). Artifical intelligence in retail — 10 present and future use cases. TechEmergence. Retrieved from https://www.techemergence.com/artificial-intelligence-retail/ (Accessed on 9 June 2018).

Fink, S. (2013). *Crisis management: Planning for the inevitable and crisiscommunications: The definitive guide to managing the message*. New York, NY: McGraw Hill Education.

Fortune.(2018). *Fortunes's world's most admired companies*. Fortune. Retrieved from http://fortune.com/worlds-most-admired-companies/ (Accessed on 29 June 2018).

Frisch, B. (2011). *Who makes the big decisions in your company*. *Harvard Business Review*. Retrieved from https://hbr.org/2011/12/who-really-makes-the-big-decisions-in-your-company (Accessed on 31 May 2018).

FTI Journal Staff.(2017). *Survey of 500 senior executives reveals the corporate crisis concerns keeping them up at night.* The economist intelligence unit sponsored by FTI consulting. Retrieved from http://www.ftijournal.com/article/survey-of-500-senior-executives-reveals-the-corporate-crises-concerns (Accessed on 5 June 2018).

Goodley, S., & Ashby, J. (2015). Revealed: How sports direct effectively pays below minimum wage. *The Guardian.* Retrieved from https://www.theguardian.com/business/2015/dec/09/how-sports-direct-effectively-pays-below-minimum-wage-pay (Accessed on 7 June 2018).

Griffin, A. (2014). *Crisis, issues and reputation management.* London: Kogan Page.

Griffiths, A., & Department for Business, Energy and Industrial Strategy.(2018). Revealed: The worst explanations for not appointing women to FTSE company boards. Gov. UK. Retrieved from https://www.gov.uk/government/news/revealed-the-worst-explanations-for-not-appointing-women-to-ftse-company-boards (Accessed on 1 June 2018).

Harding, D. (1999). *Cool dawn: My national velvet.* Edinburgh: Transworld Publishers Ltd.

Hatch, M. J., & Schultz, M. (2001). Are the strategic stars aligned for your corporate brand? *Harvard Business Review*, 79(2), 128–134.

Hillier, A. (2018). Oxfam: A crisis to end all crises. The third sector. (Accessed on 7 May 2018).

Ipsos. Ipsos Global Trends Survey. Ipsos, 2016. Retrieved from https://www.ipsosglobaltrends.com (Accessed on 16 October 2018).

Ipsos. Key Influencer Tracking. Ipsos, 2017. Retrieved from https://www.ipsos.com/ipsos-mori/en-UK/key-influencer-tracking (Accessed on 16 October 2018).

James, G. (2018). Why unilever stopped issuing quarterly reports. Retrieved from https://www.inc.com/geoffrey-james/why-unilever-stopped-issuing-quarterly-reports.html (Accessed on 2 August 2018).

Jin, Y., Pang, A., Cameron, G. T., & Pang, A. (2007). Integrated crisis mapping: Towards a public-based, emotion-driven conceptualization in crisis communication. *Sphera Publica*, 7, 81–96.

Jung-a, S. (2018). Samsung expects record profits despite slowing display sales. *The Financial Times*. Retrieved from https://www.ft.com/content/f891cda2–3928-11e8-8b98-2f31af407cc8 (Accessed on 5 June 2018).

Kalavar, S., & Mysore, M. (2017). Are you prepared for a corporate crisis? McKinsey Quarterly. Retrieved from https://www.mckinsey.com/business-functions/risk/our-insights/are-you-prepared-for-a-corporate-crisis (Accessed on 5 June 2017).

Kay, L. (2018). Corporate partners express concerns about Oxfam. The Third Sector. Retrieved from https://www.thirdsector.co.uk/corporate-partners-express-concerns-oxfam/fundraising/article/1457153 (Accessed on 7 May 2018).

Kellaway, L. (2017). Lucy Kellaway's jargon awards: Corporate guff scales new heights. *The Financial Times*. Retrieved from https://www.ft.com/content/d118ce7a-d325-11e6–9341-7393bb2e1b51 (Accessed on 9 June 2018).

Kuehner-Herbeart, K. (2018). PepsiCo's CEO and Chair, Indra Nooyi is leading the company to new heights.

ChiefExecutive.Net. Retrieved from https://chiefexecutive.net/pepsicos-ceo-chair-indra-nooyi-leading-company-new-heights/ (Accessed on 28 May 2018).

Levenson, E. (2018). Larry Nassar apologizes, gets 40 to 125 years for decades of sexual abuse. CNN. Retrieved from https://edition.cnn.com/2018/02/05/us/larry-nassar-sentence-eaton/index.html (Accessed on 10 June 2018).

McKie, R. (2015). Tim Hunt: 'I've been hung out to dry. They haven't even bothered to ask for my side of affairs'. *The Guardian*. Retrieved from https://www.theguardian.com/science/2015/jun/13/tim-hunt-hung-out-to-dry-interview-mary-collins (Accessed on 7 June 2018).

McKinsey. (2017). How to create an agile organisation. McKinsey. Retrieved from https://www.mckinsey.com/business-functions/organization/our-insights/how-to-create-an-agile-organization (Accessed on 3 June 2018).

McLaren, R. H. (2008). Corruption: Its impact on fair play. *Marquette Sports Law Review*, *19*, 15.

Morton-Clark, S. with eds. Ager, S., Stansfield, N. & Giustiniano, A. (2017). Kellaway on years of corporate nonsense. *The Financial Times*. Retrieved from https://www.ft.com/video/662356ef-1d4e-4302-8ca4–0009cfffcbc0 (Accessed on 9 June 2018).

My Supermarket. Prices. Retrieved from https://www.mysupermarket.co.uk (Accessed on 29 May 2018).

Oxfam. (2013). Our goals and values. Oxfam. Retrieved from https://www.oxfam.org.uk/what-we-do/about-us/how-we-work/our-goals-and-values (Accessed in 2018).

Pape, S., & Whittaker, N. (2018). Super superannuation special. *The Sunday Times*. Retrieved from https://www.

pressreader.com/australia/the-sunday-times/20180527/
283523681518359 (Accessed on 10 June 2018).

Patagonia. (2018). The activist company. Patagonia.
Retrieved from http://www.patagonia.com/the-activist-
company.html (Accessed on 11 June 2018).

Payne, S. (2015). *Who will influence the EU Referendum.
The Spectator.* Retrieved from https://blogs.spectator.co.uk/
2015/11/who-will-influence-the-eu-referendum-martin-lewis-
not-june-sarpong/ (Accessed on 17 April 2018).

Phillips, R. (2015). *Trust me, PR is dead.* London: Unbound.

Press Association. (2012). *Thalidomide scandal: 60-year
timeline. The Guardian.* Retrieved from https://www.
theguardian.com/society/2012/sep/01/thalidomide-scandal-
timeline (Accessed on 11 June 2018).

Quote Investigator. (2017). The future has arrived — It's just
not evenly distributed yet. Quote Investigator. Retrieved from
https://quoteinvestigator.com/2012/01/24/future-has-arrived/
(Accessed on 9 June 2018).

Reputation Dividend. (2018). *The 2018 UK dividend report.*
Reputation Dividend. Retrieved from http://
reputationdividend.com/files/6215/1939/6597/UK_2018_
report_Final.pdf (Accessed on 29 May 2018).

Rogers, D. (2015). *Campaigns that shook the world: The
evolution of public relations.* London: Kogan Page Ltd.

Roper, S., & Davies, G. (2010). The corporate brand:
Dealing with multiple stakeholders. *Journal of Marketing
Management, 23*(1−2). 75−90. (Accessed on 5 May 2018)
(doi:10.1362/026725707X178567).

Sample, I. (2017). *Study reveals bot-on-bot editing wars
raging on Wikipedia's pages. The Guardian.* Retrieved from

https://www.theguardian.com/technology/2017/feb/23/
wikipedia-bot-editing-war-study (Accessed on 9 June 2018).

Sandberg, S. (2013). *Lean in: Women, work and the will to lead*. London: WH Allen & Co.

Schwarz, A. (2008). Covariation-based causal attributions during organizational crises: Suggestions for extending situational crisis communications theory. *International Journal of Strategic Communication*, 2, 31–53.

Sky News. (2018). Thousands of donations stop as charities reveal abuse. *Sky News*. Retrieved from https://news.sky.com/story/live-oxfam-boss-mark-goldring-grilled-by-mps-11258795 (Accessed on 10 June 2018).

Stern, S. (2017). *Worried your reputation is like Bell Pottinger's? Then don't do bad things. The Guardian*. Retrieved from https://www.theguardian.com/commentisfree/2017/sep/14/bell-pottinger-avoiding-reputational-damage (Accessed on 11 June 2018).

Sudhaman, A. (2016). *What Paul Polman told the world's Top Communicators. The Holmes Report*. Retrieved from https://www.holmesreport.com/latest/article/what-paul-polman-told-the-world's-top-communicators (Accessed on 2 August 2018).

Swinford, S., & Bird, S. (2018). Oxfam boss: What did we do? Murder babies in cots? *The Telegraph*. Retrieved from https://www.telegraph.co.uk/news/2018/02/16/oxfam-boss-baffled-ferocious-criticism-claiming-critics-gunning/ (Accessed on 2 May 2018).

Teneo Blue Rubicon. (2018). About. Teneo Blue Rubicon. Retrieved from http://www.teneobluerubicon.com/ (Accessed on 9 June 2018).

The Conference Board. (2014). *The conference board CEO challenge 2014: People and performance*. The Conference Board. Retrieved from https://www.conference-board.org (Accessed on 29 May 2018).

The Financial Times. (2018). Ten-year government bond spreads. *The Financial Times*. Retrieved from https://markets.ft.com/data/bonds/government-bonds-spreads (Accessed on 29 May 2018).

The Guardian. (2017). Quantas boss tops LGBT leaders list for backing same-sex marriage in Australia. *The Guardian*. Retrieved from https://www.theguardian.com/world/2017/oct/26/qantas-boss-tops-lgbt-leaders-list-for-backing-same-sex-marriage-in-australia (Accessed on 11 June 2018).

The Good Housekeeping Institute. *Do beans have to mean Heinz?* The Good Housekeeping Institute, 2015. Retrieved from https://www.goodhousekeeping.co.uk/institute/food-reviews/baked-beans (Accessed on 29 May 2018).

The Reputation Institute. *2018 Global RepTrak — Most reputatable companies in the world*. The Reputation Institute, 2018. Retrieved from https://www.reputationinstitute.com/resources/pdf/2018-global-reptrak (Accessed on 7 May 2018).

Thoreau, H. D. (2010). *Civil disobedience*. Seattle: Pacific Publishing Studio.

Waitrose. *Products*. Retrieved from www.waitrose.com (Accessed on 29 May 2018).

Waller, D., & Younger, R. (2017). The reputation game. *The art of changing how people see you*. London: Oneworld.

INDEX